diary
of a
Hairstylist

By Emily Bakker

diary of a Hairstylist

Emily Bakker

Published by:

Bryson Publishing
Kansas City, MO

ISBN: 978-1-959665-46-5

Dedicated to my mother, and my work besties.

Without all of you I would be lost.

💕

diary

of a

Hairstylist

"Seriously!?" I exclaim with disgust. It was 8:40am and the other two stylists and I had just arrived at the salon. We had started our morning opening routine: start the wax pot, count the till, set up our station, start laundry, sanitize our tools and combs– and most importantly, try to get down as much coffee as humanly possible.

As I look up while counting the opening drawer, our regular crew of walk-ins are at the door, knocking and signaling for us to unlock it way before opening time. They have been camped out since before we even arrived, like it was a release day for the new PS5. We only had 15-20

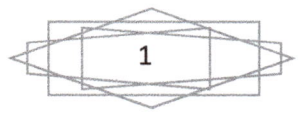

minutes to get everything set up each morning and we used every minute of it.

"Ready?" I ask the other stylists as the light flickers to OPEN.

I started doing hair at the age of five. It was 1992 and Barbie needed a new hairdo. She received sharpie lowlights, Kool-Aid pink-stained hair, and then (wanting to become GI Jane, I guess) she ended up with a buzz cut when I was done. I expanded into styling my rocking horse's yarn hair once Barbie's hair was all gone. I used a

spray bottle of water that substituted for my Aqua net, and my mom's curling iron (off obviously). You could say that the horse's hair was rockin'.

Growing up, my mother was a hairdresser, beauty operator, beautician, stylist, cosmetologist... I'm sure I missed some titles. She attended Stewart School of Hair in Council Bluffs, Iowa. The cost of attending was $1,700 at the time. After passing her exams she returned to her hometown and started her career as a hairstylist. She later went on to open her very own salon on November 17, 1988. His-n-Hers Family Salon was born. Back then, we were in and out of the salon like it was our second home. Mom was off on Sundays and Tuesdays, unless she was working at the local nursing home doing hair on her day off.

Here are some photos of my mother's beauty school days. Her graduation, the invite, balloon (proof mothers save everything), and her name tags. The different titles determined your level in beauty school.

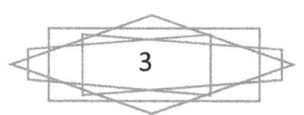

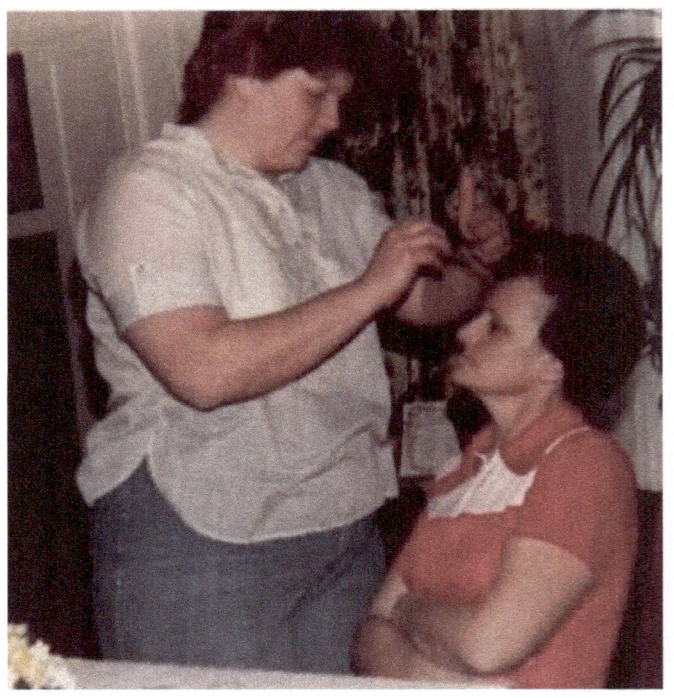

Here my mother is doing her mother's hair. Gam Gam had a perfect iron set and a yellow rod perm. My fingers hurt just thinking about red and yellow rods.

I can still remember the smell of perm solution in the air, and the salon most likely still smells of perms thirty years later. It was kind of my comfort smell. How messed up is it that I'm comforted by the smell of sulfur, gas, and eggs?

I had to be the guinea pig for all the different perm styles, Boomerang, Brick-lay, Spiral, 9-section, piggie back, up until the sixth grade when I finally said, *"Enough perms!"* I can remember being in first grade and the school receptionist saying, "Oh Emily, I just love your hair!" Meanwhile, I was thinking: *No kidding Barbara. We have the same hairstyle and pink perm rods, but you are 65 and I'm 7.*

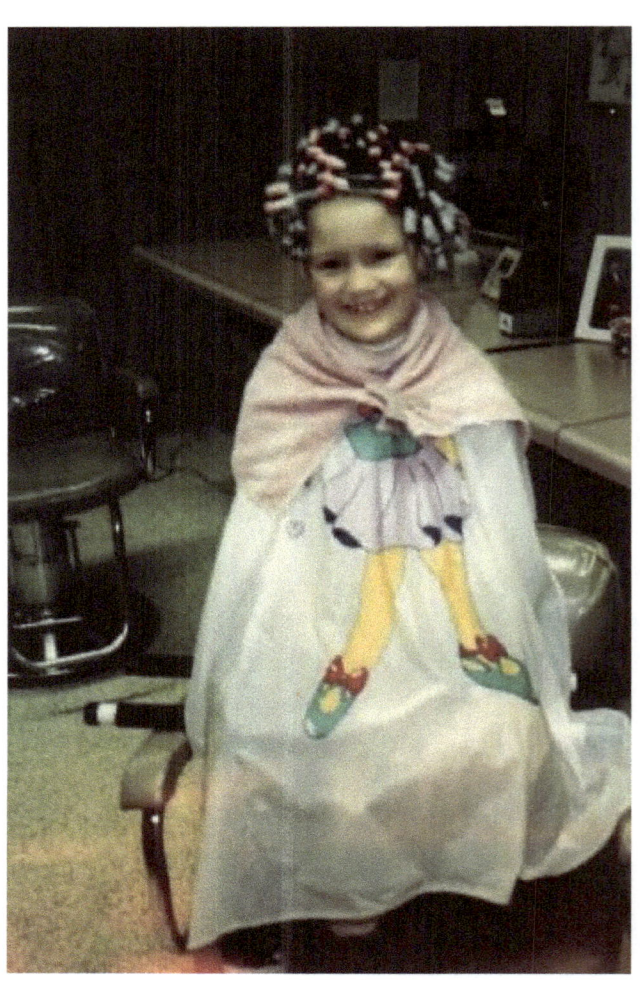

Some of the best memories of being in her salon were from Christmas. She would decorate every inch of the salon, top to bottom. There was a Christmas Tree in the giant picture window facing the town square. Later, a client's car would plow through that very same window when they left it in gear accidentally.

When the glass didn't have a car parked in it, she would use the spray frost in a can to decorate the glass to mimic snow and ice. There was a Mickey Mouse Santa on display with fluffy white batting gathering at his feet. There were, what I can only describe as beach ball Christmas decorations, hanging from the ceiling. There were lights and garlands decorating the salon, and it was fun to see it transform into a salon that Mrs. Claus would definitely go to.

Watching my mom do hair was magical. The salon was constantly bustling, with people going through the rotation of Beehive, Bouffant styles, and teased-to-perfection basketball-shaped looks. It really was a wonder to watch:

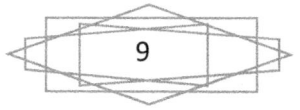

Client #1 enters, takes a seat in the salon chair, hair is shampooed, set on rollers, and sat under the hood dryer for 15 minutes, indulging in this week's Enquire magazine. Enter Client #2: Hair shampooed, set on rollers, and then under the dryer as well, except she wants to read the Redbook Magazine. It was like a well-oiled machine. Something Henry Ford would be impressed by. Client #1 now returns to the styling chair and gets the style brushed out, teased, and coated with at least a half can of hairspray. Now Client #2 is ready to be styled.

This is the art of double booking. There is zero down-time for maximum revenue. The rotation would occasionally get altered if there were perms, or cuts, but my mom handled that like the *boss* she was.

I was fascinated by how she managed to not only get the client done and looking amazing, but how she also held a conversation, asking *How's your mom? Who is hosting Thanksgiving? Have they had their baby yet? I'm so sorry to hear that, I will be thinking of all of you. Have you*

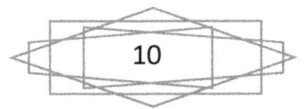

heard about Kathy? Of course, the hottest gossip always happens in a salon. Everyone knows that.

My mom (center) and her amazing friends from the hair industry for over twenty years.

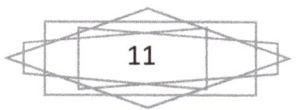

(left) My mother and aunt Linda the nurse (right)

I thought I wanted to be a nurse growing up. I saw my aunt help people and make them good as new. The only problem was, how could I become a nurse if I can't handle blood or get shots, let alone *give* shots! I just wanted to put Band-Aids on and boss people around.

Eventually, I came to the same conclusion as so many other Cosmos do. We can take care of people and make them feel better, just in a different way. We get to help with mental health, emotions, commiserate together about life challenges, try to help in difficult times or during a loss, give advice, I could go on and on. Lots of people that stop doing hair go into nursing. I think it's because the two careers take so much compassion, patience, love, and genuinely care about another human being. I love what I do. Sure, I want to throat punch people sometimes, but tell me a job where that isn't the case.

I enrolled into Beauty School in the spring of 2006 (shout out ISB). State law dictates that you must go through 2,100 hours of both hands-on (working on clients/mannequins), as well as state law and theory (textbook classes). The normal completion time ranged from fourteen months to twenty months. After that is completed, you then take the state law exams.

After I received my official cosmetology license, I applied for a position at the local mall salon. I worked there for three years, then transitioned into my second salon home. I was at that salon for eight years. I am now in my third, and final salon home for nearly a decade. I have so many stories from my life in the salon, and it would be a shame to not share them.

The inspiration for this book came from a desire to show a glimpse inside the career: what we do for our clients, what we experience, the highs and lows of the industry, the toll it takes on us mentally and physically, the joys, the juicy gossip, the life-long friendships, and the many things that have nothing to do with our actual skill or education. I don't think people in this life realize your hairstylist probably knows you more than your own family. We are the therapist, the friend, the peacekeeper, the non-judgmental ear to listen, and manage to do your hair simultaneously. It is crazy we never had mental health courses in our training. We had chemistry, anatomy, math, but never psychology. We had to just wing it.

There is something magical that happens when a client sits in our chair. They immediately open up like a can of busted biscuits. When I say they spill the tea, I mean it. I have heard everything under the sun. Affairs, deaths, pregnancies, abortions, coming out, transgender

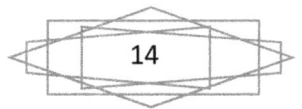

identity, fights with kids, trauma, health issues, venting about work, piercings I didn't need to know about, engagements, jail, sexual assault, cults, abusive partners, their crazy political beliefs, family drama, I could go on and on. It is an honor to have them in my chair but also a challenge to carry it all. It wears on our hearts.

So many hairdressers have health issues stemming from our line of work. It is mentally and physically exhausting. We have bad shoulders, knees, carpal tunnel, arthritis at a young age, and so many other ailments. However, we stay. Why? Just like many others in this career, we can't fathom leaving our clients. We must push through it. We have people relying on us, and we can't let them down. It feels like we have over 300 friends and family members. We love what we do. Some stories are hilarious, some are deeply saddening. This is the life of a cosmetologist.

Beauty School Dropout ♪♫

I loved watching Grease as a kid. Frenchy was my favorite character because she was fun, friends with everyone, and most importantly— colored her hair pink. She was an icon. I loved her song about being a beauty school dropout, and how she was struggling with it. She managed to make it look fun and exciting, but also scary. Frenchy's experience paralleled my own. I fully expected Frankie Avalon to break out singing "Beauty School Dropout" as I walked through the school doors on my first day.

Finishing high school is a stressful time for many. You embark on your education journey or start your career journey. You have the opportunity to make money and decide your fate. There are so many amazing trade schools now that provide fast-paced education and will get you into the workforce quickly. Everyone at cosmetology school comes for a different reason. Some had always dreamed of this career, while some wanted a way to start making money quickly.

Trade schools really are the best. I paid $14,550 total for my education in 2006. What four-year college can say the same? Yes, there were times it flat out sucked. Other times, it was the most creative and positive I've ever felt. We were able to be creative, in a fast-paced field, and make money. Win-win!

I really found myself in cosmetology school. That may sound cliché, but it helped me grow as a person. I found myself experimenting not only with my hair, but my clothing choices, my friend circle, my personality, and my humor. I figured out what my work ethic was, and my moral code. I had fun while also learning. What career really lets people experiment to the extremes like that? Sometimes I like to watch people at the airport and play "spot the cosmo." Fun hair, body modifications, tattoos, humor,

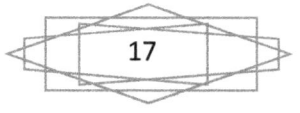

good energy, and a huge coffee in their hand. Those are the big indicators.

In the beginning of the program, we had a basic eight-week training course to complete before touching real client hair, and not just a mannequin. Then, we were ready, or at least as ready as we would ever be. In 2,100 hours, I was going to be a licensed cosmetologist. School was Tuesday through Saturday. We had the option after a certain point in our credit hours to "work" on Mondays for extra hours to complete your program quickly. I did this every chance I could because I wanted to graduate and start earning some real dough. I was in school forty-seven hours a week, and then had to work for actual money in my off time, not to mention sleep.

I felt like a new person in beauty school. I was creating a new me. I learned quickly how to strike up a conversation with a total stranger without skipping a beat. It felt so bizarre. I wasn't very outgoing or overly social at the time, so I definitely wouldn't just start talking to a random person, let alone touch their head or face.

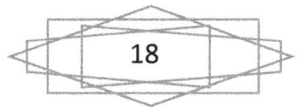

The consultation before cutting a client's hair was easy to talk through, and I felt like I had been doing it my whole life. I had been watching it my whole life. The way my mom handled talking to her clients was how I was greeting guests and asking how their mom was. Even though I have no clue who Gary's mom is.

I wanted them to know I genuinely cared what was going on in their life. The crazy part was how I could remember these random facts when they would come back. I can't remember what we had for dinner two hours ago, but I can remember the name of Diane's grand-dog that died five years ago. It was Frank. He was a Frenchie. Frank the Frenchie. Some of the best clients and the greatest friendships came out of beauty school.

These are some of my fondest memories from school.
I loved my time there.

~

The clients we had were mostly elderly.
Beauty school was a fraction of the cost of a salon
for clients. I think cuts were $5.95, and to have a
shampoo and roller set was $3.95. So, it helped us
learn but also helped them stay within their
budgets.

We often had regular weekly clients. Bee,
that was one of my weekly shampoo and set
clients. She was a feisty old lady. She got her hair

done every Saturday morning at 10am. The lady could barely see and was mostly deaf, but somehow drove herself to the school every week for her appointment. I'm pretty sure she was ninety-three at the time. She would say *back comb it more! Bigger, Bigger! Use more Fanci-full Chocolate Kiss rinse!* She prepared me for the bossy clients in the future.

The rinse she wanted was this pigmented runny liquid that temporarily toned the white hair to the color on the bottle. The names were always funny. Chocolate Kiss, Fanciful Fawn, Little White Fawn. That stuff stank so much. When the precious Fanci-full had been applied, next up was a blue generic cement gel from a gallon jug that the school supplied for styling. It was applied to her hair and we'd start rolling. I would brick lay the hair rollers like I'd been doing it for thirty-years (it felt like it) and put her under the dryer. I knew when she was about dry because I'd hear a loud THUNK! Bee's head hitting the dryer hood. She would often pass out under the dryer, and I'd think, *do I let her sleep? Did she die?* But she was resilient.

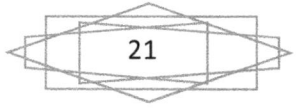

21

I'd back-comb the living crap out of her hair. Then I'd form it into the perfect ball shape preferred by older ladies, coat it in at least half a can of hairspray and put her rain cap on. Even when it wasn't raining or windy, she'd insist. We walked to the checkout counter, and she handed me fifty cents as a tip. I'd thank her and send her off in her eighteen-foot-long Cadillac, hoping she wouldn't hit anyone.

I'm guessing Bee is long gone now but I loved seeing her every week. I worried about her like my own grandma. It was hard not to get attached to the clients like family.

~

I remember the clouds of cigarettes that greeted you as you passed through the school entrance doors. So many people smoked. It would stick to your clothes, hair and skin. I think it was an easy thing to pick up, because who doesn't want to go on a fifteen-minute break, four times a day? No judgment– they were guaranteeing a break in their day– smart, really. The same smell

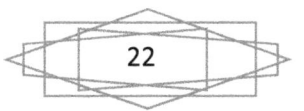

would follow the Old Blue Hairs in too, after they finished their Marlboro in the car with the windows up. It would stain their hair yellow from smoking nonstop. I wondered how strong the smell must have been in their cars.

It was so difficult attempting to remove yellow cigarette stains on hair, and they kind of vibed with the "blonde" look the yellow stain gave them. Perms that were done on the yellow stained hair would chemically react and tint it ashy-green after being permed. It was certainly a look, that's for sure. We just had to remember to educate the client. Making sure they knew how to eliminate it if they should choose to: clarifying shampoo and quit chain smoking.

~

Schools always have people with sticky fingers, and you did need to keep things locked up. That included all your salon equipment, your purse, your keys, etc. I remember one student who was justifiably upset when someone stole her phone. She walked up to darn near everyone in

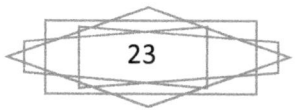

the school, interrogating *where did you put my Kyocera Slider?!!* No one knew what had happened, we hadn't seen anything. Even if we had, we went by prison rules— no narcs.

It wasn't until the end of the day when she went to take her food out of the breakroom fridge, that she realized it had been in her lunch box the whole time. She turned as white as a ghost from embarrassment. This story was retold so many times, I wonder if she laughs or cringes when she thinks about it. At least she found her phone.

~

Luckily, I have never cut anyone, which is wild and hopefully I don't jinx it. I sure have witnessed it multiple times, however. One day in school I witnessed an epic chop. The stylist had brought her client to her chair and started their consultation. Once the hair goals were established, and the instructor signed off, they began the cut.

This client had snow white hair. That beautiful, natural white-gray we all hope for when we age. As she began the cut, she suddenly stopped and said, "Did I cut you, sir?" to which he replied, "I felt a pinch, but I don't think so."

Then within seconds, blood starts filling all the white hair. He bled, and bled, and bled, like a horror film, it saturated every hair a crimson red. An instructor quickly came over and helped both the stylist and the newly red-haired client.

It was the talk of the school that day. He was fine, but I think she was rattled from the experience, justifiably so. On the educational side of this, it taught us how to properly sanitize tools, towels, surfaces, and dispose/clean blood contaminated items.

~

The first time the PA system announces your name, a million things start going through your head. You feel anxious, maybe a little sweaty, and forget everything you have learned.

"Emily, your client is here." The speaker yells over the PA system.

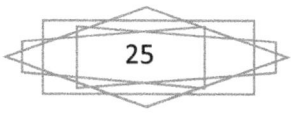

Your client is here. Don't be weird. You head to the school reception to greet them. Don't be weird Emily, don't be weird.

"Hello, my name is Emily. Come right this way."

You are mentally preparing yourself. You will be touching a random person's head for the first time when they sit in your chair. You don't know them, however now you have to strike up a conversation with them and do a thorough consultation. The consultation starts with introductions, then goals for their style, and you have to roll with it. Thinking on the fly while they are talking, planning the cut in your head. Having to say, no when the style won't work with their hair texture and feeling the pressure of trying not to mess it up. Meanwhile worrying that they won't take our advice based on their hair thickness or texture. They would end up hating it, and I never want to ruin someone's hair. You must pay attention to what they are saying while all this runs through your head.

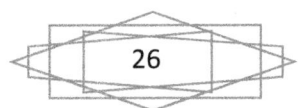

It is all in how you deliver it. Telling someone their hair won't necessarily cooperate with their style in mind is greatly appreciated I have found over the years. Be honest. Give them alternative options, or style edits that better suit their hair needs. They want your opinion, that's why they came to a professional. Getting that into my head was hard. I always wanted to give them whatever they wanted, but I had to learn the difficult lesson of saying no. You can't make everyone happy, but you can sure try.

~

Learning how to strike up a conversation beyond the consultation was strange at first. "So, how's the weather?" That is a great conversation opener every time. "Are you from around here?" That is also a great follow up question. Can you imagine sitting in dead silence during your whole service? Talk about awkward. I am sure there are people who do in fact prefer a silent or quiet service, but it helps when clients voice their preference for silence.

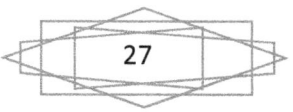

I would much rather have a client communicate that, versus having to wonder if they are upset with the service. That is exactly where my mind would go. Now, I can walk into any room, and confidently strike up a conversation with anyone. Cosmetology school gave me those skills.

~

Once you complete a certain number of hours, you are given the chance to apprentice at a salon. As an apprentice you did tasks like sweeping hair, helping clean, answer phones, shampoo clients, and anything that wasn't a chemical or cut service.

It was a cool opportunity for a student to get the vibe of working in a salon. Seeing the interactions with clients and getting to assist stylists in their appointments was empowering. I felt like I was part of the team, and they appreciated the help. It simulated what I would experience with my license, a few short months from then. The way the stylists all worked

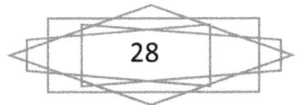

together, and the fun atmosphere of the salon also encouraged me. It wasn't a stuck up, mean-girl salon, which was a fear many of us had in the back of our heads the closer we got to graduation.

One day, while helping at the salon, the phone rang. It was a guy calling to ask about getting waxed. He wanted to know if the salon waxed men. I said, "Of course, why wouldn't we?" He said, "Well, do you do Man-zillions." I was holding my laughter in because I had never heard it called that. I didn't know if he was serious or just being funny. I asked him to hold a moment and I would confirm that it was offered.

The stylist that was next to me took over from there. She said matter-of-factly, "Hello, yes, we offer that service. Back, crack, and sack, we do it all!" I burst out laughing so hard. I love that about our industry. You can always trust us to be honest but have a giggle about it too. *B.C.S., we do it all!*

~

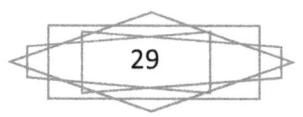

Everyone's hair was constantly changing in school. We all went from having hair down to the middle of our backs, to looking like we stuck our finger in an electric socket. Seriously. Then the color education started, and we not only cut all of our hair off but fried what little was left of it. We had fun and would learn every time from whatever experiment or mistake that ended up on our heads.

I attempted to find pictures of all the crazy hair I had but clearly, I knew it was bad because I have zero pictures of the wild styles.

~

Lice. It is bound to cross paths with you at some point. Might as well be while in school learning. It happens. Kids have sleepovers or share helmets at baseball. Parents don't notice, and kids don't either. It is commonly the stylist who notifies them. It's stressful to have to deal with, and makes people feel gross or dirty.

In actuality, lice like clean hair, not dirty. When the hair is greasy, the lice can't grab onto

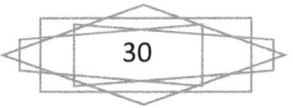

the hair shaft. It is simply too slick. The average lifespan of lice is up to 30-35 days. An egg takes 6-8 days to hatch, and a female can lay up to eight eggs per day.

Are you itching yet? They breed fast, which is why it is often discovered suddenly. It happens in only a few days, and only takes a small exposure to make a new home on your head. Now, there are so many ways to remedy the situation quickly and effectively, and many of the myths about lice have been disproven.

When a mom comes in wanting me to take twelve inches off their daughter's hair, that's the first red flag that they have lice. The second, is that the client is itching incessantly. Many stylists will refuse service if the client has lice. So, parents try to get a lot of hair cut off before treating it at home, which makes it much more manageable to clean.

It all comes down to educating yourself about lice and educating the client. It is as simple as telling them the correct products to eliminate it and reassuring them. Yes, it sucks, but it doesn't have to be the end of the world. There were many cases like this when I was in school, and I can confidently say I am well trained in dealing with lice.

~

We all remember the emo bangs. Maybe you're still rocking them or have since retired them. Either way they were a big lesson for me in school. I had a teenager come in for a bang trim one Saturday. It was a bang trim yes, but all her hair was pushed and swished into these bangs. The side part where the bangs began was behind her ear. Let's be real– it was a teenage comb over.

So, I began combing and trying to get a grasp on where these bangs started and ended. As I began to comb, I immediately felt a tangle. I kept pulling the comb, and her head would pull too. This tangle was deep in there. But she didn't say anything about it hurting or having a sensitive head.

Finally, I had to lift the front section of bangs because this tangle wasn't moving. It was at

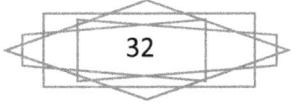

that point I realized, every time I took the comb to the hair, the teeth of the cutting comb were getting snagged on her freaking eyebrow piercing! But she never said *"ow!"* She just sat silently. I felt awful and kept apologizing over and over, but she was unfazed. Her head was yanked so much, and the whole time it was my comb stuck on that damn barbell. I don't know what was more shocking, that I didn't rip out the piercing or that she was mute about it. Note to self, check for facial piercings.

~

I remember my first long hair spiral perm. This lady had hair past her butt. It was thick, and gorgeous. Why would she want to fudge it up with a perm? Either way, she was mine for the next five hours. I didn't mind perms, but on this length, girth, and rod size (get your head out of the gutter), this was going to be a task. I started at the bottom of her head slowly and neatly curling each half-inch section onto the perm rod. By the time I had placed the last rod, I had been rolling with my arms above my shoulders for 4 hours. My shoulders were *dead*. My back was collapsing. I was ready to call it quits on the whole career.

I finished the service, and it looked great. She was happy. I walked her to the front and thanked her, then returned to my station where I contemplated my life. I was so tired and sore I couldn't even talk.

Then I heard the intercom call out, "Emily B. please report to the front desk." *Fuck me, what now?* I coaxed my legs and body to shuffle up to the desk where a group had gathered. The teacher handed me my tip that the perm client had left. $100. I. Was. Rich. All my pain, frustration, time, and energy went to something that this client loved so much, she tipped me $100 on a $40 perm. To show extra appreciation and gratitude like that made me feel emotional. I decided to not throw in the towel that day and keep pushing. Thank you, whoever you were.

~

I get really upset when people discredit or look down on stylists like they didn't have to go

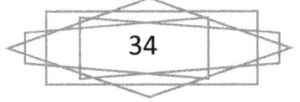

to "real college." We took anatomy, chemistry, biology, basic math, among other courses. State law was an entire course of its own as well. Learning how to disinfect properly and have sterile equipment was a must. What happens if we cut someone? How do we clean that up? What happens if their skin has a reaction? What ratio do I need to use to color correctly?

So please don't ever discredit us for not going to a four-year university, or not being educated in a traditional setting. We have so many opportunities because of this career and are living our best life. *Haters gonna hate.*

~

Salon Vibes and Tribes

In the salon, many of us are "trauma bonded," according to my therapist. You have been to hell and back together. You work as a family, not as coworkers. You all survive the day or die trying. Ride or die. The way you come together and work as a team makes or breaks the salon. It's like being at the end of a shift as a server. Everyone is exhausted. You have been on your feet for nine hours running all over the restaurant, you look around, take a big gulp of your better-be-free Diet Coke, and see all the other employees weighed down by the same kind of exhaustion. We made it through the shift together. It's that kind of support we rely on.

When the whole salon is miserable, and staff feel unappreciated, it will end in the failure of the salon. No client wants to come into a toxic environment or listen to the staff bitch. That's how you can tell if the salon has good vibes and happy stylists. If clients sense negative energy, or unhappy stylists, they turn and run in the other direction. Like a spooked animal. It is ultimately up to the owner, and the creative souls that build their career together under one roof, to work together to succeed.

The golden rule— treat others as you wish to be treated— should be ingrained in employers and business owners as well. It goes both ways. When employers take advantage of their employees, they leave. Owners, supervisors, franchises, and corporations in every industry are all guilty of it. Please don't get on your high horse and say, "Well I was there once, it's grunt work and I get it sucks, but someday you…" Forget that! I would never treat an employee as my less than equal. I would do the same that I ask of them. You want to work Black Friday in the salon at midnight? Exactly. Want to work on Christmas Eve? Again, no! How about being open until 9:00 PM? Why yes, I would love to never tuck my baby into bed at night. There are so many employers that have no problem committing their staff to working holidays, weekends, and inconveniences that they themselves would never do. All these feelings and manipulations build, and build, until one day *poof!* We are all gone, and you wish you had made different choices for your staff. The following stories are the good and bad of salon environments, the tribes we have found, the effects that trickle down, and what makes or breaks you.

~

I have worked at three different salons. That may not seem like a lot for over eighteen years in the business, but it means I found good salon tribes in each one of them. My first set of salon besties was right after graduating from cosmetology school. There were several girls I had been in school with who liked their salon. So, I applied, and boom— I was a real-life licensed stylist, making real money.

It was a strict environment in the salon at first. It was filled with hours and hours of the

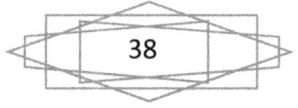

franchise's introduction and safety videos. For example, did you know you can't just jump off a ladder? Even better, you can't wax someone with the temperature on high. Duh! All of these seemed like common sense, but I guess not everyone always has that.

I really enjoyed my manager there. She tried to haggle for fair treatment, wages, and always had our back. She made sure she was there for cleaning, crappy schedules, inventory, I mean all of it. We were such a strong team, because she was a real leader.

My time ultimately ended when the corporation started doing write-ups on any employee that didn't meet a sales quota. After three write-ups, you would be terminated. The number of new clients I had was completely out of my control. The company was desperate for money and kept raising prices. A client could come in October and their cut was $38, then in December it would be $46, and then in March it was $52. I don't blame the clients at all for not

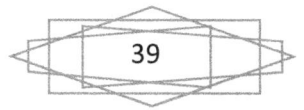

returning. Even for someone not on a budget, that is a crappy way to run your business.

This was a way to get the numbers up and to help stylists hit their sales goal. You made minimum wage until you hit your sales goal. Then, you were switched to a commission pay scale, which was great if you had a large clientele. As a newbie it was awful. It was a way for the company to get away with not paying minimum wage or overtime. That was how it was back then. Because so many stylists had quit, and we were working such long hours, it was averaging $2 less than minimum wage at the time. So, you would work 50+ hours and be making $5.25 per hour. No one can live on that.

Even though I loved my friends that were coworkers, I could not stay any longer. That company has since left the entire state, and everyone up and left within the month. I should have left sooner, but I stayed for them, and I like to think they stayed for me.

~

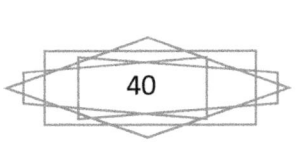

I went to my second salon because I had heard good things about it from other stylists. The salon network is amazing in our community. We communicate with each other through Facebook groups, salon supply houses, and being active in the field. We can share information to stay clear of certain employers or encourage others to make the leap to a different company.

I needed benefits, fair wages, and a positive environment. I had that for a good amount of time at my second salon home. It's always good until it's not. You get wrapped up in the clients, the other stylist, and you get used to the changes that keep coming at you little by little. I was at this salon for a large portion of my career. I felt like I really grew as a stylist there. They had a massive clientele, and a variety of services to offer.

Four years into working at this salon, I was promoted to manager. I was tickled pink. I was on top of the world. I realized later it was more paperwork than anything hair related. How to write people up, how to manage the schedule—all

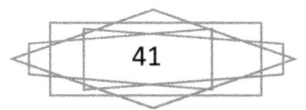

41

useful things. It was educational, that's for sure. As a bonus, I didn't have to watch a bunch of dumb safety videos like the last salon, instead they had a short in-person training. They trusted that we could use our brains.

The job eventually became too much with me working long hours and having a baby at home. So, when my son was two years old, I resigned. I told my work besties a couple days before so then they knew it was coming. I felt like I owed them that. I was crying because they were upset, and justifiably so. I was leaving to go to a salon where I would be self-employed. I already had an established network of clients, and I found the next salon family to move into.

I think this salon really helped me learn and grow as a cosmetologist, but also as a human. We met so many different people. So many crazy people, and some of the best people we could have asked for as clients. They had employee parties and tried to pay it forward to the stylist. It would have been nice in hindsight to just take that money and raise wages instead of an elaborate

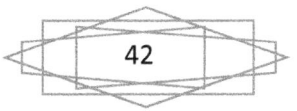

event. Not my company, not my choices. They did know how to throw a party though. I appreciate them for what they did for me in those eight years.

One of the parties… Chippendales.

~

So began the next and final chapter in my salon career. My current salon tribe. In a massive open concept salon, you had the opportunity to rent a chair out on the main floor which was laid out similarly to all the other salons I had worked in. You also had the option to rent a studio to decorate and fill however you liked with a private door, and everything you needed. All I had to do was pay the owners once a month for my space.

It really was a whole new concept to me. Overseeing my own schedule, clients, and life. I was learning how to manage myself. They were so gracious when I started. I was terrified after quitting the previous salon. I was leaving all my friends behind, and the guaranteed income. My fate was in my own hands. That can be terrifying but also so rewarding. I quickly got to know the other stylists in the salon, everyone was so welcoming. It was professional, yet laid-back. It was a salon full of people with their shit together. I guess if you didn't have your ducks in a row being self-employed, you would quickly sink. So, it made sense that everyone was friendly, drama-free, and well-rounded. There has always been room for me to grow in my skills, and I was surrounded by others who lifted everyone up and were encouraging. They wanted everyone to succeed. They had free education all the time. They didn't have to do that in a salon rental set up, but they did.

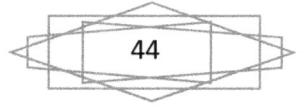

This salon was updated, bright, clean, professional, and I felt a sense of pride telling everyone this is my salon home. At one of the previous salons, things were run down, and it felt like you had to fight to the death to get a lightbulb replaced.

I remember we needed to have the lightbulbs in the bathroom replaced at a prior salon. There were 4 bulbs and one by one they were going out. I asked maintenance over and over to replace them, and the response I would get was, "Well, there is still one bulb working right?"

…and sure enough the lights all finally went out and we had to use a flashlight to go to the bathroom.

That was what I was used to dealing with. Not having a functioning air conditioner. Having a hole in the ceiling that corporate didn't want to fix. Broken washers and dryers. I could go on and on. So, now, to be in a salon where, if any issue arose, they fixed it within the hour, was shocking. It was luxuries like that. How pathetic, a luxury was a light in the bathroom.

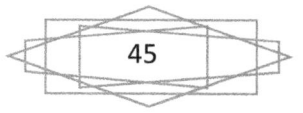

We also have the best cooks in the world if you ask me. We regularly have someone bringing in gourmet salads, and homemade dressing for all of us "just because." We have homemade desserts, chocolate, cookies—someone is always cooking something. We essentially have our own farmers market in the summer. Someone will bring in apples, then peaches, then make salsa from their own garden. We show each other how much we care by spoiling one another. We take care of each other like family.

The universe and stars all aligned when my past work besties contacted me and said, "All right, how are we doing this?" They were at the point in their lives as well where they needed control of their schedule and lives. Three out of the four of us were all pregnant at the same time so we were all in a similar situation with kids, and hectic lives. I shed a couple tears as one by one they started transitioning over the years from the previous salon into our current salon home.

I was on cloud nine thinking "Is this real life?" How could all of us finally be under one roof?? Then COVID-19 hit. I was six years into being self-employed. During COVID-19 we were not able to work for nine weeks. It was a mess. Financially, emotionally, and physically. The owners of the salon never charged any of us rent while we were shut down. In total we had three full months that they covered for us. Who does that? A salon family, that's who. No one had a clue what was going to happen, or what reopening

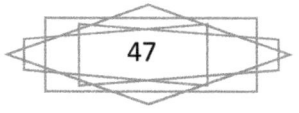

would even look like. However, we knew we would get through it because we were together, and we still are.

Freaking COVID-19

In early 2020 the world came to a halt. There was a new mysterious virus that was taking lives and becoming a full-blown pandemic. Everyone was affected by it. The panic, lack of knowledge, and fear everyone had was terrifying. In our state, we were shut down for nine weeks. For many of us that were self-employed and didn't have unemployment, it was very challenging. There was some assistance offered to select individuals, and then others that received nothing. It was an interesting turn of events for all our clientele as well. Many still had to go physically into their office or place of work. They still needed their hair done. However, we legally couldn't perform services for those nine weeks.

It was interesting to hear how clients navigated that time. Spouses cutting each other's hair, wax jobs at home, how-to videos on Tik Tok. I would receive messages from clients asking which box color I used. As if I'd been using Clairol box color on them from Walmart! I used a professional color that is formulated from scratch. I get that they were trying to come to a solution, but everyone was rocking that gray and outgrowth. It bonded us, so we all looked wild. I heard of stylists doing hair for their neighborhood in their garage, some still going into a salon, and just trying to figure out how to make up the money they were losing, while simultaneously trying to not get sick.

In the beginning of the pandemic, we were all flying by the seat of our pants. We didn't know what was going to happen when the governor allowed us to return to work. Was this layer of material over my mouth going to protect me? How was I going to deal with mandating it in the salon? Just because the governor made it a mandate didn't mean clients were going to respect that. So, we enforced the rule: wear the mask, or turn around and leave.

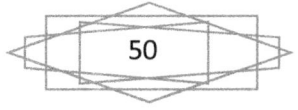

I remember the day the governor announced we could return to work. I didn't know how I was going to feel. I missed my clients and the money, but was it safe? At 11:04 AM when the announcement went live, my phone blew up. It was like everyone had their phones ready to contact us as soon as possible. I had seventy-two text messages, five emails, and forty-one voicemails, all within one hour.

Wearing a mask did suck. It was hot, claustrophobic, and I felt like I touched my face even more while wearing it. I felt especially bad for the people wearing glasses that steamed up from wearing the masks. Shout out to the medical professionals who wear them constantly.

There were multiple clients at the start of the pandemic who would come in with two N95 masks layered up, and a pair of gloves on, they were so nervous. Then, just two months later wanted to protest the mandate and thought the entire coronavirus was not even real. I was shocked by the number of scientists and doctors I suddenly had in my chair, because I knew nothing

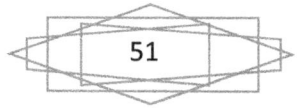

of how the virus works, and left it to the ones who actually studied the subject. Who am I to tell anyone whether their actions or opinions are right or wrong? However, I was disturbed by the amount of people who needed to be reminded to wash their hands well. That should have been a habit solidified by kindergarten. As Kevin McCallister said: "Wash your hands you filthy animal!"

We already practiced all the disinfecting and sanitary procedures in the salon, according to state law. So, when asked if we had a huge adjustment after reopening, we stated that the mask was the only real adjustment. Salons should already be sterile places because they are constantly cleaned.

There were many positive things that came out of coronavirus procedures. It was no longer "weird" to wear a mask or ask your client to wear a mask when you had a cold, and vice versa. I now wear a mask at the airport, and I am not singled out as strange. It became a normalized practice, much like in many other countries

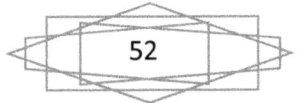

around the world. I will take a COVID-19 test if I don't feel well, now that tests are available almost everywhere you can be preventative about spreading it.

I had COVID-19 the week before Thanksgiving this year. I thought it was allergies, but I still tested. Boom, positive. I didn't want to expose anyone, especially my loved ones who were at the greatest risk of exposure. The holidays often feel like one big COVID-19 party these days.

I lost three clients to COVID-19. It was sad and terrifying. The virus was unbiased—out for everyone. I am so thankful my immune system was strong, and when I did get sick, it wasn't deadly.

~

First COVID-19 Vaccine

Clients

I am so lucky to call so many of my clientele friends and family. People can suck—don't get me wrong—but not these precious souls. They put their trust in me entirely. It really is a privilege to get to do what I love with people who appreciate, trust, and respect me. I can get a message saying, "What would you say about me going copper?" My response would be "Hell-to-the-no, Shelbi! You love your blonde and don't like reds and warmth." This is an actual response to my client. They know I will tell the truth whether it's what they want to hear or not. I sometimes say it gracefully, and other times I don't. I know them, their willingness to maintain it, their color and length preferences, or dislikes.

That's one of the benefits to being in a long-term relationship with your stylist.

The best clients are the ones that are flexible and respectful. They understand life happens outside the salon. Sometimes appointments need to be moved, kids get sick, stylists themselves are sick, or even an emergency or a loss. When I step out as I leave the salon for the day, I am instantly thinking of a million things I need to do. Just like every human, we have a lot on our plates. We all need a mental break, we need a massage, a hug, our favorite music, or even to go scream at the sky. We need to catch our breath too. Please know we see you and appreciate your understanding and grace.

Here are some stories from clients trusting the process and those who push us to our limits.

~

I had a client once that came in for red and I mean *red* hair. I performed the service and matched the goal photo spot on. Like, I nailed that shit. When I brought her back from the shampoo

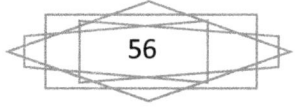

bowl, she saw it for the first time. At this point, the client started crying. She said that it was nothing like the photo, when in fact, it was exactly like the photo. Three other stylists stopped in to look as well. It had been a process and they wanted to see how amazing it turned out.

The client began to realize that it was the correct color, she just didn't like the color on herself. I offered to color again at a minimum of four weeks out from the first color, for an additional fee. She agreed. Two weeks later, she called me to cancel the second appointment, telling me about all the compliments she received. She wanted to keep the color.

Sometimes these situations are frustrating to deal with when clients aren't immediately happy. However, they often love the color once they get validation from others. Some people need others to notice, or to acknowledge them. All she needed was confidence. I gave her a whole new look and she rocked it from there on out. Stylists can completely change the whole life and mood of a client if their hair is amiss. My heart is happy

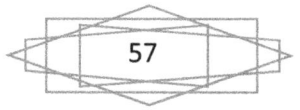

when clients have an amazing hair day and love their hair.

~

Client pet peeves bring us back to the beginning of the book. This story starts, like many others, with people lined up waiting at the door for us to open. We were hustling, trying to get everything set up and ready for the day.

Looking out the front door at them, most would think, "Oh that is so nice people are there and waiting for you! They must really love your stylists." Yes. But no. There were almost always 2-3 guys waiting at the door every morning. Why? Because the salon was walk-in only and they *had* to be first.

While we appreciated their business, we always felt rushed getting set up for the day with someone watching our every move, and annoyed to have people banging on the door before opening. Please don't repeatedly bang on the door twenty minutes before a business opens. Don't wave me down to come to the door and open early

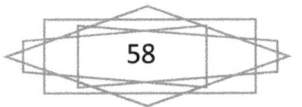

for you. I don't own this salon. I'm not paid to open early either. In fact, I might wait until two minutes after just to piss you off. Openers in any business have a checklist of things to complete before opening, that ensure the day starts successfully.

Don't ever mess with employees like that. Anywhere. Any job. They already have enough shit on their plate without you telling them how to do their job. Be patient.

~

When clients become lifelong friends, it's magical. It's like the universe plopped them down in your seat specifically. Some change the course of your life, and vice versa. I get goosebumps when I imagine if someone else had taken that client. What if I had never met them? I wouldn't know because I would have never been granted that opportunity.

Everyone is unique and clients know almost immediately if it is going to work out with a new stylist. Before we even touch their hair

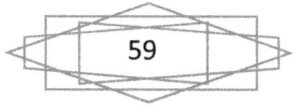

really. It's a vibe, an energy, a personality, and it's unique to each of us. Some clients will remain in a professional client-stylist relationship. Others you can't help but befriend. You see into their lives, their interests, their jobs, and you genuinely connect. One of my closest friends is only in my life because of hair. It was by chance that she called the salon and was assigned to my chair—like destiny. It feels like that all the time. The stars align and we meet the coolest people and hear their adventures.

One of the top five badass clients I have ever had was a Nike rep named Kathy. Kathy smoked three packs a day, gave zero fucks, and wanted a mohawk mullet. With lightning bolts shaved in as well. I was like *dibs on you Kathy*! When she told me what she wanted, I understood the assignment. I asked her why the change? She said "Life is too short. Why not? Just Do it." *Mind blown!* But really, Kathy was right. It was from that point on in my career that I followed that mind set. Life is short. Try something fun and take a chance. What's the worst that could happen? Hair grows, and time shrinks. Just do it.

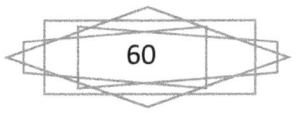

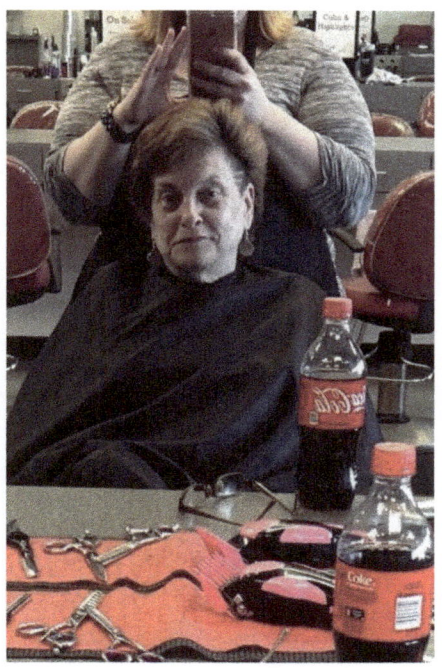

Badass Kathy

~

It can be so hard to set boundaries with clients. You become friends, follow each other on social media, you see them more than any of their personal friends and even family. It's okay to have friendships with clients, but it can be hard seeing how lonely and isolated they are, and you don't have the time or energy to give back. I feel like the scum of the earth if I don't make coffee dates, or message back and forth like I'm their only outreach or friend. Our care extends beyond the salon walls. My therapist says that it is healthy to have boundaries, but I can't help but want to support and be there for these people.

Compassion is part of the career. I have had clients that have lost their job and couldn't afford to come in for their hair. They were still interviewing and trying with no luck. I wanted them to feel confident and strong. Sometimes their hair helps them feel like their best self. A clean cut. Gray hair covered. A great style. You can't afford it? Then come in and we will get you fixed up. It is on me. If we can't support one another in a time of need, then shame on us. We are all human and need to look out for one another. I love being active in our Community and helping wherever I can.

~

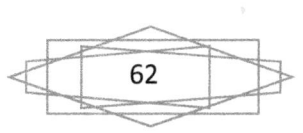

Our salon at an event for homeless veterans. They received hot meals, a shower, medical care, clothing, haircuts, and so much more. Thank you to Kathy (far right) for all these connections that enable us to help so many people in our community.

Breast Cancer Event 2018

"A Night to Shine"

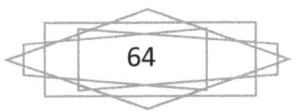

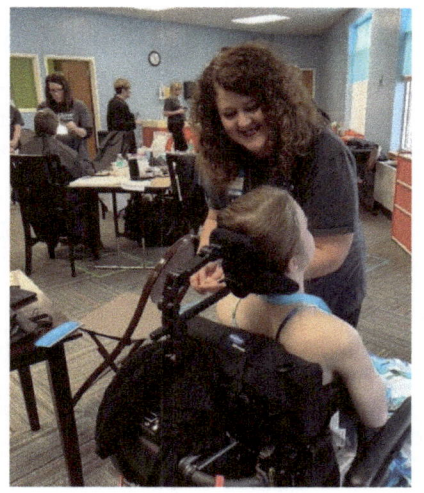

"A Night to Shine" prom hair

One of the best moments with a client is when they tell you they are getting married. It is a special time in their life, and they trust you to help them look their best on the big day. It's such an honor to be part of it.

There are so many moments I have been lucky to share with brides, grooms, and their families. Behind the scenes, the first looks, the father and daughter, bridal party moments, the tears, the final placement of the veil, and mom seeing her baby all grown up and glowing. I often hold the hand of the mother of the bride. Feeling her trembling, watching her daughter walk out to see her father for the first time. As the hairdresser, I am witnessing this Lifetime Movie Special right in front of me. I could go on and on. It is so freaking cool to see all these intimate moments. I cry every time.

Then there is the flip side of the wedding day where you are chasing down groomsmen to trim their neck lines and making sure the wind hasn't sabotaged the perfect bridal hair. Having plans for if it rains or is humid. Getting granny in at the last minute because she wanted to feel special too. Going through 1,000 bobby pins and getting multiple curling iron burns on all my fingers. Listening to the mother of the groom tell me about how in 1969 weddings cost *blah blah blah*. Bridesmaids that want their updo changed, and you don't have time for it. Making sure no one has on a tight collar shirt because it will mess their hair up when they go to change into their attire. Things like that are what we have going on in our heads.

... and I love every minute of it.

~

It has been a special experience for me to support my transgender clients on their life journey. Trans clients are such special clients. I love being able to give them a look that matches their true self. I have had trans men, trans women, and non-binary clients. I have worked with them before transitioning as well as post-transition, and it is so freaking cool to see them with a whole new personality, and level of confidence just from

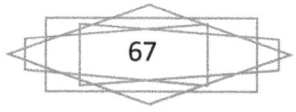

changing their hair. The ability to give them affirming hairstyles, helping them learn the new techniques for their new hairstyle, and providing product education is a privilege that I don't take lightly. Someone may not have taught them how to use a curling iron or blow dryer, and I'm able to provide that level of support.

We change lives. We encourage. We support. We give them a safe space to just *be*. I would be lying if I said I was perfect and never messed up a client's pronouns. I always correct myself and apologize immediately. We are all learning, growing, and changing together.

~

Shout out to the industry professionals that truly enjoy the high maintenance client. Because that's a hard pass for me. As you move through your professional career you start to notice services you prefer over others. For example, I am most passionate about color services, blonde color specifically. That is the clientele base I have grown the most.

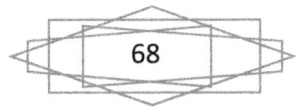

Those that take the path of barbers, precision cuts, shaving, and higher maintenance services, I have so much respect for you. I know myself, and I would not do well in that area. I don't have the patience, or the steady hands. I am not rubbing a client's shoulders at the shampoo bowl. A hot towel? Salons don't even pay us for maternity leave. I am not toweling or rubbing anyone. period. If I did, I would have gotten a masseuse license. Those are services that typically come along with being a barber as well. Many seek out them for the pampering services.

Seriously, barbers really are so skilled at their craft and talents. Barbers are the hardest working people, I think. Physically, but also mentally. Those select clientele are devoted to those amazing skills. I can replicate color services and techniques without even thinking about it. Now, if you asked me to duplicate a fade, line up or shave, you would see me running out the door. That's what I admire about the different types of hair service careers that we have. There is a niche for every passion, and every specialty.

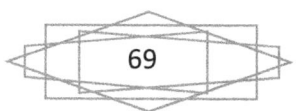

It is really rewarding to pause and look at your clients over the years. Some clients bring their whole families to you. Some had their first haircut with you, and now they are graduating. Then they bring you their babies for *their* first haircut. They grow up so quickly just like our own children and families. You are part of their family. You do the hair of their mother, grandma, aunt, uncle, cousin, co-worker, spouse, and you become so involved in their lives.

Akin to the intricate weaving of a web, referrals lead to more referrals; all of them connected, branching off into multiple directions. It is ever growing, always changing. It's beautiful. I feel like I have my own mini town within the walls of my salon

~

Oops!

The most common question asked as soon as someone finds out I'm a cosmetologist is, "Have you ever messed up someone's hair?" The answer is yes. We all have at some point or another. It may have been something major, or something only we knew about. We all learn, and we all grow. These stories are from myself and other stylists I have witnessed.

~

It was a busy Saturday at the salon during the back-to-school season. The reception was packed with irritated kids and parents. Most kids hate getting their haircut. If you haven't ever experienced this, count your blessings. Parents are annoyed they have to wait, and we are annoyed there is nothing but children's haircuts on

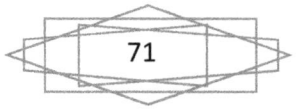

71

the books for the day. It is one of the more labor-intensive, tiring times of the year. Any stylist or barber who says they don't have PTSD from back-to-school cuts is full of shit.

I remember asking my mom how she did children's haircuts with them constantly moving. She responded with, "It's easy Em, you grab the hair and cut it." Now I can understand that, but at the time I was questioning her advice. The more time went on I learned that they move, I grab a chunk, they move again, and I grab a different chunk. It was like a dance. You just kept moving and cutting, just like mom said. Distracting things always helped. Like counting the Giraffe spots on the cape or watching their favorite show on their parent's phone.

Ok, back to the "oops." We were all busting our asses that day, kid after kid. I had an eight-year-old boy in my chair.

Dad yelled from the lobby, "Do whatever." OK, sir.

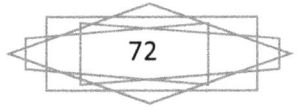

I asked the child, "What would you like to do?"

He said, "I kind of want to grow it out a little." Well, pops over there wanted us to trim it at least a little. So, at this point we agreed on a longer clipper guard for the sides and decided to trim the top just a bit. I put my longest clipper guard on, which was a number six, or ¾ inch of hair left. So, it was taking maybe a ¼ off his hair in total. I was about halfway around the head, and it happened: the guard I had on my clippers broke and flew off just as I was going in to take another pass of his hair. The guard landed five feet away on the floor in two pieces. My friend working stopped her cut and looked at me. I looked horrified at her. Then we both looked down at the floor and saw the sad, broken clipper guard.

That poor kid. When the guard flew off it only left the bald clipper blade and that took the hair down to the scalp. There was nothing I could do to try and salvage the cut. I wanted to laugh and cry at the same time. It wasn't an impatient child moving and bumping it off, it wasn't in my

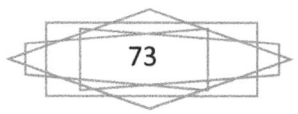

control, but regardless, he left looking like he'd just enlisted in the army. Oops!

~

The first salon I worked in was in a mall. We built a lot of our clientele from people roaming around the mall on a Saturday. One day, a woman in her early twenties walked in for a haircut. She had insanely thick hair. The stylist took her back to begin her appointment. I was chilling in my chair waiting for my next appointment, so I was able to witness the "Great Thinning of 2007" that would unfold.

She brought the woman back, draped her in the cape, and headed to the shampoo bowl. The normal routine. She then walked her back to her station to begin the cut. Thirty minutes later she was almost done with the service and the client said, "Can you please thin it some?" She happily agreed and grabbed her texture/thinning shears. She then moved to pick up a massive chunk near the exoccipital bone on the back of their head. This is typically where we start thinning hair, it is

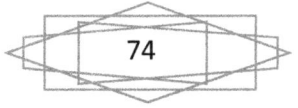

an area above the nape but not towards the crown or top layers of hair. The thinning shears are designed to only remove 20% of the existing hair, so it is a soft and gradual transition. Sadly, not this time.

Chomp! We all heard the steel blades slice closed. The stylist quickly excused herself saying she had cut herself and walked to the back room (This is sometimes an excuse we use to go to the backroom and collect ourselves if something goes wrong). So, I promptly followed her to the back to make sure she was okay, and she said, "You guys I just chopped a massive chunk out of this girl's hair!"

What happened was, her shears were all jumbled in a drawer, and she had grabbed her *cutting* shears, not thinning shears, by mistake. A well sharpened pair of shears will cut through wet hair like a hot knife through butter. From that one quick snip, they now had about a 4x2 inch hole in the back of their hair. The stylist shrugged in the backroom and said, "I'm not telling her." That is

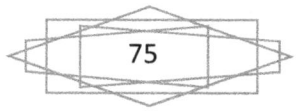

exactly what happened— she finished styling her hair, rang her out, and sent her on her way.

She never called to complain and never came back. I still wonder to this day if she noticed. She must have, right? Oops!

~

It was August and my bestie was coming into the salon to get her hair done. I was super excited because we were going to use a new color line that the salon had just transitioned to. She was pumped, I was pumped. She was meeting friends at the state fair that night and was going to have a fresh, new color to show off. We decided on a color formula that was like the previous line and I went to mix up the new color.

After we completed the processing time of thirty minutes, I noticed it looking rather purple. No big deal, because color oxidizes and can look totally different when the product is on the hair versus when it's washed out. It can be scary to the client when it looks darker or the wrong tone. Again, that is totally normal. Her color had a

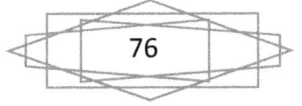

violet base in it, so I was confident it was just oxidizing purple.

That is until the water started rinsing it off at the shampoo bowl and it was truly plum purple. Like *purple* purple. I said, "Uhh, I'm anxious to see this dry..."

To which my bestie says, "Anxious-nervous, or anxious-excited?"

I looked at my friend that was working, and my face must have been communicating *oh shit*, because she helped me find a solution while I was panicking.

In the end, I removed the purple and re-colored it. It came out close-ish to the goal color. But how could that have happened? Well, the mixing ratios were different from the previous color line, and I didn't use the new ratio of 1:2. One part color to two parts developer. Instead, I used 1:1 and it was even more concentrated violet. Lesson learned. Thank goodness it was my friend!

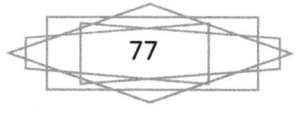

~

Fake it 'til you make it. Those are some solid words of advice. It was a busy Saturday morning at the salon. A mother and her daughter had just walked in asking if anyone knew how to braid. Half of the girls were experienced braiders, and the other half were not as confident. Not a problem, I greeted them, and walked them to my chair. The cheer mom asked for her daughter to have two Double Dutch braids. All the cheer team needed to have matching hair. Now, I know how to braid, but I was thinking, "Double Dutch what?"

So, having no clue what the hell a Double Dutch braid was, I made up some excuse to go to the back room and quickly YouTubed a video on Double Dutch braids. I was panicking that I had just signed myself up for something I couldn't do. Come to find out that it's just an inverted French braid—a big braid on the top of the hair. A smaller example is a cornrow. Thank goodness someone had a video online. Thank you, baby

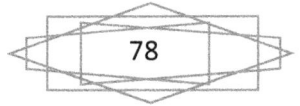

Jesus for YouTube. We are still learning every day.

~

Have you ever heard of a Flowbee? It is essentially a vacuum with a clipper on the end. It sucks the hair in and will rip, pull, or cut the hair. It was painful, never consistent, and hilarious to see in action.

One day this gentleman comes into the salon and looks like he had just come from a funeral. In fact, he kind of had. His Flowbee had died, and he was so upset that for the first time, at the age of fifty he had to go somewhere for a cut. His consultation was thirty minutes—for a cut! Rule of thumb is, if the consultation is more than twenty minutes and you are still not on the same page, then you will never make that client happy.

I could tell he was full of anxiety and kept repeating how he couldn't find replacement parts on eBay, that they no longer make them, and then repeated the story all over again.

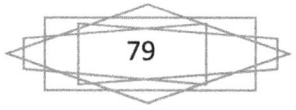

It was a short shag hair style that he wanted, which was straight forward. The amount of hair that hadn't been cut or was left uneven, floored me. It looked bad. When I said it rips hair out, I meant it. One chunk would be eight inches long next to a one-inch-long strand where it broke off. How could this be what he wanted but shorter?

We finally started, he paid, and then left. I never saw him again. I have no doubt he found replacement parts and fixed his Flowbee. That was one of the top five messed up cuts I have had to fix or replicate. Yikes!

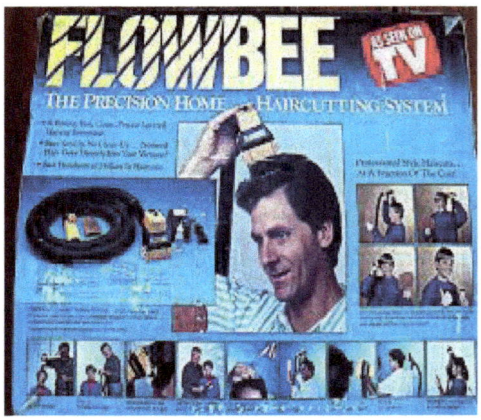

This is the funniest kid-cut-their-own-hair story. It was at the first salon I worked at. It was a slow Sunday. A Father suddenly came rushing in with his three-year-old. The panicked Dad asked if we could fix his kids' hair. The child had a three-inch circle of buzzed bald hair on the front of his head. He was so darn proud of himself too. He proudly strutted across the salon showing off his handiwork. His father shrugged and said, "He must have found scissors and, well, oops." We had no other solution except to buzz it all down. The poor kid looked bald.

The little boy was pissed we had messed up his haircut job too. It was so harsh with that chunk missing that all I could do was disaster control.

Kids cutting their own hair is always hilarious, they are so proud of themselves. The dad paid us, thanked us, and they went on their way. About a month later, the dad reappeared. Same kid, same chopped spot, same proud little boy. Dad explained he asked the three-year-old to show him where the scissors were, and he proudly

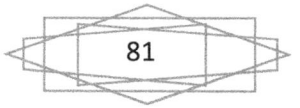

walked his dad to the master bathroom. He went to the vanity, opened their drawers...

You think you know where this is going, but I promise you don't. He dropped his hand into the drawer, and it reappeared with an eight inch long, vibrating...

Nose hair trimmer. Bet you didn't see that coming! A nose hair trimmer wielded by a three-year-old was the weapon of choice. I am so glad he chose to come back to us again and tell us this hilarious story. He knew we would get a chuckle. Oops!

Senior Care

with the Blue Hairs

We really are lucky to care for so many seniors. We are sometimes the only good appointment of the week. Other appointments being the doctor, a funeral, a pharmacy, or the hospital. There are so many of our loved ones that are likely to see their hairstylist more than their own family every week. We are their constant. We set them up for the week with a fresh wash and blow out. We almost always hug, throwing a "Love ya, hun!" out there for good measure.

We refer to them as Blue Hairs sometimes because they would have yellow tints in their hair from smoking or general minerals from their well water or city water. We could help them lessen their yellow stained hair by using a blue based shampoo to counteract the yellow and neutralize the color. The color wheel in action. The problem after they left was how they continued washing their hair nonstop with the blue shampoo and slowly tinted the hair a pale blue. They loved it, and hence the name "Blue Hairs."

My relationships with my Blue Hairs will always be treasured. They love seeing us and we love seeing them.

~

One of my Blue Hairs that comes weekly for her shampoo and blow out stands out the most. Barbie. She is the sweetest woman. She has been coming to the salon for around twelve years now. She used to live about thirty minutes from where I grew up in rural Iowa. We would always try to play Dutch bingo (finding out who you know in common, and the area of the Danish community they were from). When you grow up in a small community and can relate to their history, it helps them open up. They feel valued and relevant in the conversation. They feel heard. They can go

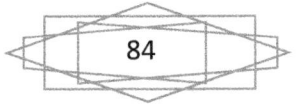

down memory lane and I know exactly what they are referring to. It is beautiful.

She always asks, "What's the scoop ladies?" to the group of stylists she sees every week in the salon who chit-chat with her. The salon is her version of Enquire Magazine (basically TMZ, for the kids reading), where she learns all the new and happening things in the world.

She asks, "Have you dumped that boyfriend yet?" and "How's your mom?" Again, even though she doesn't know my mom, she still asks. Sometimes clients will ask if I have favorites. Yes, I do, and Barbie is one of them.

~

Something we have to watch out for with our Blue Hairs is when a client is in a bad situation with their health. We need to contact someone because we are concerned and want to make sure they have help if they need it. I wish I had created an intake or client contact form to have updated annually earlier in my career. I should have done that way sooner than I did. I need to know who you would want me to contact in an emergency. We witness early signs of Alzheimer's, and health concerns in general. We pick up on traits that have changed or mobility issues that have declined.

What happens if they have no contact listed? It could be that there are no living family members, or perhaps they have removed themselves from their community. We often see them more than anyone else. More than family, more than their doctor, more than friends at times. To all my Blue Hairs: please make sure your stylist knows your emergency contact preference. We worry. You are our mom, grandma, friend, and client. It is a package deal.

~

I recently had a client get moved into assisted living at a senior care facility. It was abrupt but she needed help quickly. She was a weekly shampoo and style client. I have gotten to know this gentle soul over the last six years. She

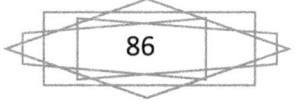

was single, divorced, and never had any children. She had a horrible childhood. She was almost drowned by a parent at the age of five but survived and went on to live with her aunt. The aunt that raised her was basically Helen Keller. Not kidding. Her aunt was 80% blind and 100% deaf.

Because of the trauma of her childhood, she couldn't have water near her face, or she would panic. Therefore, she has always needed outside help for shampooing and washing her hair. She could shower but she just couldn't get past the fear of water on her head. She had siblings that were older and looked out for her the best they could. It was good they stepped in when they did. She'd started referring to her parents as living when they were long gone. She started forgetting appointments. She was falling, losing her balance, and getting more and more confused.

As I've said, we see these souls more than their family most of the time. We hear their ailments and struggles. We aren't medical professionals, but we also know when we need to

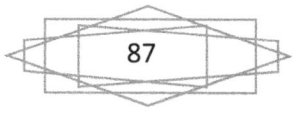

step in and let the family know something seems amiss. I miss her, and I miss all my seniors that move on into the next stage of life. I hope they know how much I care for them and miss them.

~

What happens when our clients do pass on into the next life? Well, sometimes they still need their hair done just one last time. Family members will reach out to their stylist to style their hair in preparation for their funeral, so they can rest in peace with great hair.

This is something my mom did for some of her clients. She had a special hair tote she would take with her to the funeral home. Scissors, irons, spray, combs, etc. Maybe the men needed a haircut at the time of their death. She would do that too.

There are so many stylists that do this. I haven't been asked yet but if I ever do, it will be a hard decision. How would I even get through it? I wouldn't be able to see past the tears to get the job done.

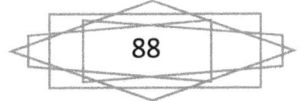

Blue Hairs make our lives better and we are forever connected. They would bring me cookies, garden veggies, flowers and really good hugs. It is so special. I feel that I've had twenty grandmas and eight grandpas in my life.

You're FIRED!

Everyone in the industry "fires" clients. Sometimes there is a definitive reason, like canceling at the last minute repeatedly, or not showing up to an appointment. Those that don't respect our time by always being late, aren't tolerated. Sometimes it is a friend. Sometimes it is a family member. Sometimes it is a client you have had for fifteen years.

In some cases, we can't keep up with the number of clients we have, so we must scale back our clients or part ways with them. We do it out of necessity and for the survival of our careers.

Sometimes it feels like a breakup. Then there are other times where you think, *bitch, bye! You don't respect my time, or profession. Why would I continue to schedule you?* If one person cancels, doesn't show, or is late and you are unable to make that money you were planning on, it breaks down to $50-150 a week at a minimum and over a year between $2,600 to $7,800. That's just one person. My bills don't stop because people don't show up.

Many stylists have adopted the system of keeping a payment on file or requiring one on their booking site. This helps recoup some of the lost income. I have had people say, "Well I won't be back!" after enforcing late or no-show fees. OK Karen, I have a waitlist of other clients willing to swoop in and take your spot who do respect my time. So, bye Felicia. Here are some of my most treasured "you're fired" stories.

~

In this case, it was an issue of differing personal morals. I should start by saying I do reserve the right to not serve a client. This doesn't happen often but there are times you must part ways.

I should describe my studio before I begin this story. We each get to decorate and set up our

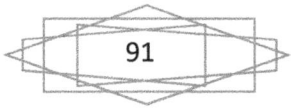

studio however we like. Most independent stylists or salon owners personalize in the coolest ways. I have a fun, bright and happy studio. Rainbows are literally everywhere in my room, I have flamingos all over, glitter in the wall, paint, fun sayings, and a bright, cheery mood that reflects me as a person and how I live my life.

So, I have "Karen" (everyone I fire is referred to as Karen or Chad) in my chair and she is a consistent client. Never late, and she always pre-books. Score, right? Or so I thought. We are about six appointments into our hair relationship, and she starts discussing a family member and how they no longer speak.

I said, "Well people have boundaries, and we must respect that."

She promptly cut in and said, "Well, he is mentally disabled."

I respond, "I am sorry he has that challenge in life," and I leave it at that.

She pushed the topic further and told me "Well, he is gay."

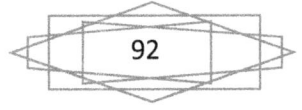

I responded, "Okay, and?" What did that have to do with his disability? Well don't worry because she clarified for me:

"He is gay because he is mentally disabled. He was born with something wrong, and his brain is obviously not right and that is what made him gay."

I was stunned. How could a person be so mean and hateful? She explained with such a casual tone, it was just a matter of fact to her. How sad. Do you not see the rainbows, the stickers, and pins for causes I donate to? My room screams inclusive and *ally*! I literally didn't say a word for the rest of the appointment. Dead, awkward silence. Yes, we all have the right to our opinion, but this is not it. I stopped trying to rationalize with crazy people a long time ago, so I blocked her and never saw her again.

~

This is one of my all-time "chef's kiss" client-firing moments. The day started off busy, it was Saturday, and we were kicking ass and taking

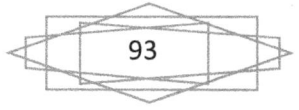

names. We had several color services on our appointment book.

In walks Karen. This particular client was the type that was never happy. The client that sees red and their hair is white, the client that wants to go from ten years of black box dye to platinum blonde in one appointment. In this situation we didn't really get the luxury of saying no to clients. We were kind of forced into taking them.

This time it wasn't Karen herself receiving the service, it was her daughter. Her daughter was the complete opposite of her mom. She was the kindest and most appreciative girl. So, the stylist started doing her consultation for the service. They thoroughly went over all the things she wanted, the color goals and the cost. We had a consent form signed for the color, price and realistic options listed. The mom left and returned a couple hours later just as the daughter was finishing up. The daughter loved it. She kept thanking the stylist and saying it was better than she could have ever hoped for.

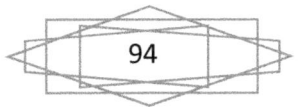

Mom walked over to the stylist mid conversation and said, "That isn't what she wanted, and I am not paying for it."

The daughter was mortified. It was gorgeous, and exactly what was signed and approved to have done. The daughter was begging the mom to pay the bill. It was a busy day, and the waiting room was packed so you would think that the scene the mom was creating would be embarrassing for her. No, it just fueled the fire more.

At that point, I was over this whack job disrupting the entire salon and trying to weasel out of paying her bill. This was the third time she has pulled this. I walked over to the front desk where the argument had migrated to. I left my client mid-cut to come over and back up this stylist. I stayed scary calm, so she would know she'd fucked with the wrong people.

I calmly said, "Okay, you have two options, and I am leaving it entirely up to you Karen. I don't care which you pick, but I just want you to know you do have options. Option one, I

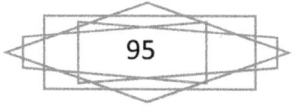

think it's the best outcome, but again you decide. You can pay the bill you signed your consent for. Plain and simple. Now Option two, I really, really hope you pick option two. I call the cops and we let them handle this. You understand that is theft, correct? Anyway, just let me know. We are going to go back to our paying clients now."

I started to walk away, and the daughter quickly pulled money from her own purse to cover the bill. Her Mom was so pissed!

Mom yelled, "Why did you do that? They wouldn't call the cops!"

The daughter calmly responded, "Because she did what I asked, and I love it."

They beelined it out of there. I really wish she had chosen option two. Fired!

~

Creepers. They are the worst. We have had them at every salon. There are always a couple of them. This creeper was the kind that wanted to stare into your eyes as you shampooed

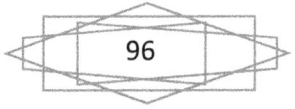

them. PSA, please don't keep your eyes open and stare at us, it's weird. Anyways, he is one that reminisces about his "wild swinger" days or running naked. Like, gross Chad. No one wants to hear that shit. Especially not if we have to touch your head.

There were so many Chads and creepy Karens. Creepers almost always get blocked. However, there have been times where they change their number or call from other numbers. Then you start pressing criminal charges for stalking.

There's one individual that always calls almost all the salons in our greater metro area. They are inappropriate, they give false identities, and when they do come in, it's the goosebump chills vibe. My experience with this person was, they came in wearing a short dress, and started to grab at their genitals and moan while I am shampooing them. *Nope. We are done. Get the F out.* Now, was I trained on what to do if this happens in a salon? Absolutely not.

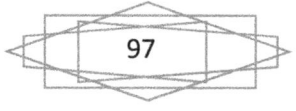

Unfortunately, this was just one of many creepers. We have to stay safe, and make sure we are paying attention to our surroundings. Have a plan in place for if you are ever in an inappropriate or unsafe situation like this. Make sure you are never alone in the salon. If you need to be, then lock the salon doors. This sounds excessive until you are in the situation. It is bound to happen when we are in such close proximity to the clients. Stay Safe.

~

Did you know that you can fit a full-size bottle of Captain Morgan in the pocket of cargo pants? I'm not talking about JNCOs either. One night, two other stylists and I were just fifteen minutes from closing, when this man walked in. I greeted them, and said, "Hello, how can I help you sir?"·He was slurring his words, and stumbling. He managed to get out, "haircut." I asked his name and he proceeded to pop open the liter of captain from his handy cargo pants and took a big ol' drink. He mumbled something about shotgun shells, and I was like damn these cargo pants are really packin'.

I immediately knew we needed to get this gentleman some help, whether it was suicidal thoughts, or self-harm. I didn't want to scare him off so I said, "Give me a couple minutes and I will be right with you." He took a seat, and I discreetly walked into the back room and contacted the local police. I explained the situation and that he just needed help. The police arrived maybe ten minutes later and were so cool about it. I mean, they totally took his ass to jail, but they weren't confrontational. Once they got him outside, they searched him in the parking lot, and he had three more bottles of booze on him. Crafty man.

~

You know the feeling when you do the right thing, and it still backfires? That was the case for us one evening. We had closed the doors at closing time, and a minivan whipped into the parking lot. A kid dashed to the door and started pulling on it.

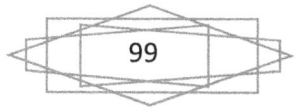

My first thought was that he had been in earlier and forgot his coat or hat. Kids are always leaving things behind. So, I unlocked the door, and by this time Mom was out of the car as well.

I said, "Hey bud, did you forget something?"

Mom cut the kid off, "Uhhh no we didn't forget anything, he needs a haircut!"

I replied, "Sorry we are closed for the night."

"No, you aren't! The clock in my car says you are open for one more minute. I demand you cut his hair!"

The child was mortified. He kept saying, "Mom, I told you we needed to leave earlier!" She completely ignored him, and demanded we cut his hair. I was thinking to myself, it is going to take more time to get this crazy lady out of here versus just cutting the kids hair. So, I did. I took the child back; cut his hair and he was in tears embarrassed. I felt so bad for him.

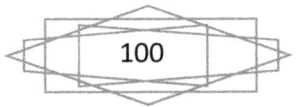

100

We headed to the checkout counter and Mom paid, leaving no tip, of course. Then wrapped up the crappy moment by saying, "I want your manager's number!"

No prob Mom! One moment… I spun around, doing a 360 and greeted her.

"Hey, I am the manager. How can I help you?"

She wasn't a fan. What else could I have done? Absolutely nothing. She was looking for a fight. We had not only opened up after closing, but then still cut his hair. So, please tell me what there is to complain about. I'm waiting...

~

Sometimes sadly we can no longer handle the massive amount of clientele we have, so we have to cut back. Our bodies literally break down. I have had to cut back my own schedule due to partially torn rotator cuffs, and two bad knees, and arthritis. For others, it may be carpal tunnel, back and neck issues, etc. Please try to have grace with

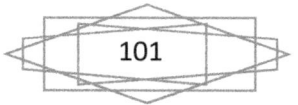

us when we must set limits for ourselves and cut back. We will connect you with great referrals. We will make sure you are taken care of.

It is very hard to do this. It feels like we are firing them, but we aren't. We are just guiding them to the next great stylist. It breaks our hearts to cut back. So please don't think we take the decision lightly.

~

I once had a client that texted me on a Sunday and asked if they could make an appointment. I did not respond as it was my day off. I typically respond within twenty-four hours and like to schedule when I am in front of my books in the salon. My day off is my own. I must have boundaries.

This client had texted me at 7:00 AM about an appointment, and an hour later I got another text from her. This time it read, "So I guess you are not going to take me as a client anymore." All of this because I didn't drop

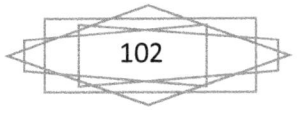

everything I was doing to get back to them within the hour, on my day off.

I was so irritated. How dare they get on my case about not responding on a day off, let alone a Sunday. I couldn't wait until Monday to respond because I was *mad*. I sent a reply stating just that.

"How dare you accuse me of ditching you. It is my day off and I don't respond because I am not in the salon, in front of my schedule."

I know I didn't have to explain myself, but is it right to assume you should get a response in under an hour on a Sunday, and then snap back with that attitude?

Well, she had one thing right, she was no longer my client.

~

That's a Wig

Social media filters, and wigs can really get people's hopes up. Clients often love to show us pictures of their goal hair via Pinterest, Instagram, or Google. They can show us the photo during the consultation to give a vague price quote, or tell them if the photo is realistic with their hair texture, density, length, etc. This can be a great tool during consultations. It can also mislead what is actually happening in these photos. For example, social media filters can change the colors in the image to be more vibrant, the appearance of unrealistic colors, "one day" transitions from black hair to platinum blonde.

If a stylist ever tells you, they can get your hair from black to blonde in one sitting— they are full of shit. Well, they could do that, but your hair would be all over the floor from melting off. Anyway, please don't think we don't like pictures

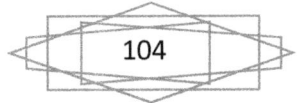

or goal ideas, they can be useful, just don't be upset when we tell you it has been photoshopped, it's a wig, that it can't happen in one appointment, or is not ideal for your texture. Like they say, Insta vs Reality.

No Filter

Filter

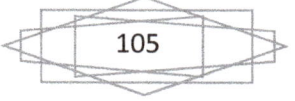

See the difference? One is more vivid and almost appears to be orange at the top. The unfiltered image is darker and deeper. They are both beautiful colors, but one is a lie. That is what we try to explain to our clients when dealing with enhanced images. We want to educate.

I refuse to put my reputation, education, and name onto a walking billboard if I don't think I can achieve it. Stylists, it is ok to say *no*! Clients, it is also okay to tell us no, and leave. We all have the right to choose what is best for us. This is part of what we are taught to do. Consult, advise, educate, execute.

The things I love about filters and wigs are that you can see what you would want before jumping into bangs again or taking the leap and cutting all your hair off. Wanting to try a new hair color? Try it out on any one of the hairstyle filters or buy an inexpensive wig. They can be great tools and can function as a base to work off. AI filters aren't just for making us look like we have makeup on, or a silly smile. These are

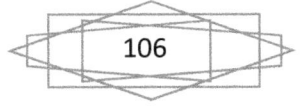

106

amazing tools that we can utilize vs taking the leap and then having instant regret.

The customer is not always right, but sometimes the stylist isn't either. That is why consultations are so detailed. It benefits both of us and ensures a smooth appointment. My favorite question to ask a new client is, "What do you not like about your hair?" A lot of the time, that can answer almost every question I have. Communicate so we can create!

Wigs can help so many people. Whether it is hair loss from chemotherapy, alopecia, nervous hair pulling ticks, or even a needed confidence boost. Extensions are a different form of wigs too. They can help add thickness, or they can cover up hair loss. There are so many amazing hair accessories to help clients feel their best.

~

One of the bravest girls I know is my client "E." She is fierce, confident, and happy to educate anyone who asks about her alopecia. Her amazing mom even made business cards with

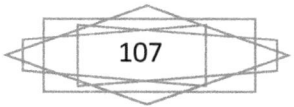

links to information, so she could hand them out to anyone who asked about alopecia. She was proud to educate other students if they asked and is such an icon. I know my twelve-year-old self couldn't be as brave.

The day had come for us to officially buzz off all her remaining hair. I say, "all" but, it was down to just the hairline left. I was afraid I was going to get emotional, shaving a twelve-year-old's hair off, and in turn I would make her upset too. I didn't know how to prepare myself mentally for the appointment.

When she arrived for the appointment, she set the mood/vibe. She walked in with a big smile. She was ready to rock no hair. She was over trying to hide the bald spots, and over having to deal with it coming out in clumps.

She said, "Now I can have the fun colors of hair I always wanted."

At that moment, I wondered, what if she took charge and got to be a part of cutting it all off. It

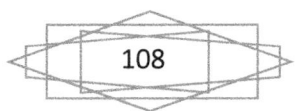

would be something she could have control over, unlike alopecia.

I said, "Do you want to take the first swipe with the clippers?"

She responded, "Can I??"

Bestie, of course you can! So, I handed over the trimmers to her. I explained the way to hold them, and that they can't cut you, so don't be afraid. Then, like Patrick Swayze and Demi Moore in Ghost (but in a non-creepy way), we took the first pass through her hair together.

When I tell you I bawled the second they left, girl. I was so relieved it had gone well: her outlook was amazing, her parents were supporting her, she was going to be just fine. I learned about places that host alopecia camps. I learned about the amazing community she had to support and educate her. She even educated me that day. She set her intentions and made it such a great experience for everyone involved. That is one cool twelve-year-old.

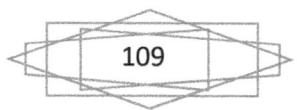

~

I love vivid colors. Ask anyone I have had in my chair. You can just tell by the smile that doesn't leave my face when I'm styling new pink hair, galaxy colors, or hair that looks like fire. I really love transitioning someone's hair into fire. Reds flowing into orange, then making the tiny tips of the hair yellow like the sun. Sometimes these colors stay well, and other times they will only last 4-6 washes. Don't be surprised if we insist waivers be signed, specifying the longevity of the color. We want to be brutally honest about expectations.

It can also be a massive challenge to achieve these beautiful colors. You can explain over and over that the color could fade, or that we can't determine the exact color until we decolorize the existing hair and see what your hair will let us achieve. If we can't get the pre-existing color removed, then it is not realistic. That is where we have to make a decision on whether we should alter the plan for the color. We may consider a vibrant wig to give you the exact look you want.

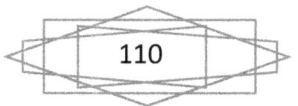

Possibly we compromise on some vibrant extensions to achieve the look and maintain the integrity and health of your hair. There are so many reasons to love the options of wigs, and extensions. They can give instant results.

~

At my current salon, we participate in a lot of volunteer opportunities. We had an amazing opportunity to donate our services to helping cancer survivors get ready for a photoshoot. The clients were selected by the Breast Cancer Foundation for this opportunity. The photo shoot was for their marketing materials, and the survivors were going to be showcased.

It was such a humbling, emotional, and beautiful two hours. I had a woman who had survived the odds, and then had to face cancer yet again. As a two-time-cancer-kicking-woman, she was ready for a cut and maybe, just maybe, color. She was seventy-eight, I believe, and had never had her hair colored.

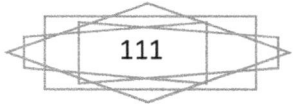

She said, "Well the lady from the foundation said we get to come and have a makeover, so here I am." She was just excited for the opportunity.

Her hair was the most beautiful shade of white. Not like silver white, but the color of snow. It was stunning. *How in the hell was I going to tell her to color this beautiful hair?!*

Well, I did. I said "You have the most beautiful shade of snow; you know what would really turn some heads? *Pink!*"

She said, "oh my goodness, what will my Bible study girls think??"

I said, "They are going to want it when they see how good you look with it!"

It was freaking amazing! You could tell this was one of the top-five craziest things she had done in life, those three foils of pink. During our time together she told me about all the amazing moments she had experienced since being a survivor. The grandchildren born, the weddings, the family gatherings, so many things she was

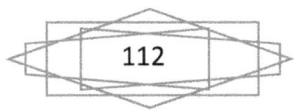

grateful to still be here for, and now this photoshoot.

They had an event later that month for all the volunteers, and survivors debuting their photoshoot they had done. It was amazing. I was so incredibly lucky to be a part of that day, and that special woman. It's moments like that when I truly love what I do and am grateful to have the opportunity to impact people's lives.

All the volunteers at the survivor's benefit

Wigs can really help with your confidence. Not only for a fun night out, or event, but for helping clients who have hair loss. There are so many options these days for hair treatments.

Not all wig clients suffer from effects of chemotherapy, there are many other reasons stemming from health, genetics, nervous ticks, and many more. It is estimated that over 50% of women suffer from hair loss. For men it is 85%. Some clients suffer from alopecia, thyroid issues, hair loss caused by sedation during surgery, cancer, genetics, menopause, stress, even from COVID-19.

There are so many things that can be stacked against you when it comes to hair loss. Wigs, falls, extensions, and toupees are all great solutions. Please don't ever hesitate to ask your stylist for help with any of these solutions. Hair is often one of the first things people see on one another. We should all be able to strut with confidence from getting an amazing hairdo.

~

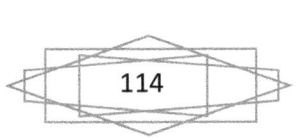

The Tea, Sis

I am sure you have seen TikTok videos, or memes saying, "If you wronged me and my stylist knows, they definitely don't like you." To be honest this is 100% true. I hear about the cheating, the abuse, the betrayal, the juicy shit— but I can't tell a soul. Like I said in the beginning, it is like an unspoken sacred rule between stylists and their clients. I have to keep my mouth shut. It's hard because some of this stuff is *really* juicy. I don't need to watch a reality TV series because I'm living it. Of course, there's a consistent "to be continued," at the end of every appointment, to be picked up in six weeks at the next one.

I often have both partners in my chair and must pretend I am hearing this information for the first time. Sometimes, I feel like a doctor, because of how seriously I take client confidentiality. I haven't taken an oath. It's an unspoken law: *keep your mouth shut as long as everyone is safe.* So, it means I have to listen to Sam tell me about the divorce and the heartbreak, having already listened to Steve last week tell me that Sam cheated on him. Things like that. It gets hard keeping stories straight. I try to be a therapist for both sides, coaching them through life, cheerleading, all while doing their hair.

There are things confided in us that we can't ever repeat. We are the only people they can tell. They know we offer a listening year and a chair to cry in with zero judgment. Whatever they say, stays between us. It is that sense of safety that allows them to open up. The things they share... sometimes I forget what I am doing. I can't tell you how many times I must label color bowls, so I don't lose track when Kay tells me about the hot and heavy night she had.

You and George did what *last night? I'm going to have to google that one. Sounds like*

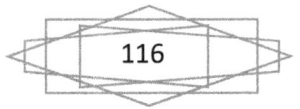

flexibility is key. Now, was I weaving that last foil or slicing?

I'm not gonna lie, it fills my cup. These are some of my Tea stories over the years.

~

Some of the best client tea comes from the nurses. As I said earlier, I have a soft spot for nurses. They deal with the public, hygiene, mental health, and illness. So, when they want to vent about their day, I am all ears. We can relate.

There are times when they share horrifying shifts they had. Things that they can't unsee and now I can't either. A patient defecating and smearing it all over the walls because, "Elvis told me to." Children coming in an ambulance from abusive homes, the ER waiting rooms being full of homeless people with nowhere else to go, people overdosing in the waiting room. So again, I listen, and nod. I can't imagine the trauma that they bring home every day.

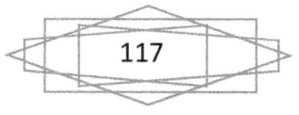

The most typical stories from nurses are about the people who come in with something stuck up their butt. I had a nurse tell me once about a ninety-year-old man who came in with a whole light bulb up there. To be clear, I am not judging anyone for putting things in that special spot but, please, be safe. Tie a string onto it or something. It seems almost like a challenge to see how much fits up there. Nurses and doctors are there to help and you should seek medical help if you really are in a pickle, or if the pickle is in you!

~

On the topic of pickles, I have lots of clients who work in the healthcare field, as I mentioned. They need to vent or complain just like anyone else would.

When people start to lose their minds, it can be sad, but it can also hold stories of humor. The amount of times a "pickle" is whipped out in front of nurses, aids, and staff seems to be very common. The men and women that go through Alzheimer's or dementia can regress to adolescent

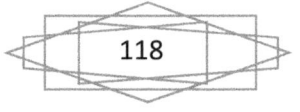

thinking. For example, whipping out that pickle because they want to let the world see it. They have lost that shut off switch which allows them to censor themselves and reminds them what is decent and indecent. So very often my client's appointment begins with,

"Guess how many pickles I have seen this week?"

Or "Guess how many times I have caught patients getting naked together?"

Apparently, STDs can even run their course through retirement facilities. Things I didn't need to know but are still interesting to hear. The hairstylists in retirement communities probably have some wild stories too. There is never a dull moment, that's for sure. Again, the tea is piping hot.

~

Another great source for "community tea" comes from my realtor clients. They know what's really going on in your community. Want to know

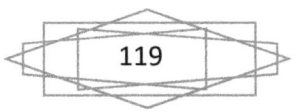

what happens in the vacant lot across the street? They know. Want to know why that coffee place closed? They know.

Want to know what kind of events are coming up? Better yet, want free tickets to an event? They will hook you up! Seriously. I have been given concert tickets, movie tickets, golf event tickets, theme park tickets, etc. I could go on and on. They truly are great at getting everyone out in the community and very knowledgeable about the goings on around town. They know how to sell to the community because of their profession and they are so good at it.

~

When I was a kid, I really, and I mean really, wanted to know what was happening to that old lady on the TV, vocally shampooing her hair in the shower? Do you remember that commercial? It was a woman shampooing her hair and having just the *best* time. So vocal. I wanted, no, I *needed* that shampoo. I was going to feel whatever that was with my hair, too!

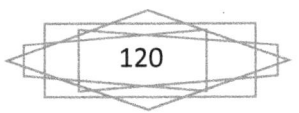

My mom almost shit a brick when I asked her if I could get a box store shampoo, aka a non-salon professional product. She refused to buy a product that was filled with wax, and poor-quality shampoo. It was "against her personal morals." Well, now I get it. She knew what I did not. The sHmerbal shmEssence (for fear of their retaliation) shampoo commercial was full of crap. It was filled with shower moments I wouldn't experience for years to come and left me with waxy residue in my hair.

There is a reason the shelf life is longer on those products in box stores. They are not held to the same standard as the products I retail in a professional salon. You have to invest in the right products to have your own shower scene.

~

The way I could write for a soap opera after just the first year of cosmetology school under my belt. I worked with so many fun people. The conversations they had going on with their own clients were personal, dramatic, devastating,

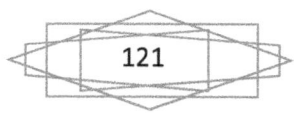

and hilarious. It was always reassuring that every other stylist had the same connection to their clients. We all provide a safe space to vent the juicy stuff, the sad moments, and the laughter. We boost them up. They trust us.

If you literally just sat in my chair for the first time, the comfortable environment, the vibes, allow you to share your soul. It's beautiful. Now to be clear, if you tell me some crazy stuff, I will keep your identity sealed, but I will likely tell my partner, and my bestie, at least some of the juiciest stories.

It is important to have a great support system, period. I come home exhausted, drained, and verbally vomit all the drama, and tea to my partner. They listen to me, they try to understand my frustrations about the violet toner going ashy and how I should have used a 0.18 not a 0.81, and they nod and listen, clueless to the language I'm speaking. They try to keep up with my rambling about a client being thirty minutes late, and having to attempt to notify every following client,

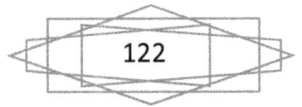

because suddenly I was behind for the remainder of the day.

They have to sit by while I disassociate. They ask me a question and I can't focus or listen because I have eight texts for appointments, two emails for appointments, nine voicemails, and I must get back to Sara about whether I can reschedule her, but first I need to confirm Liz's appointment. It never seems to end.

They listen to my complaining, and they share in the excitement of the amazing stories I have every day. They are my hype person, my mean girl, my confidant. Just having someone to vent to about your day whether it is your dog, mom, plant, whatever it is—you must let it out. I am so thankful for that.

~

Have you ever had your nose waxed? Waxing is the most satisfying time of my day. It is a wax service that involves removing the hair from the first ¼ inch of a client's nostril. You perform this by using a wax stick (popsicle stick)

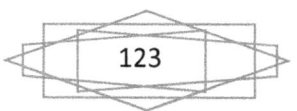

and dipping just the tip of the stick into the hot wax. Then, you place it inside the tip of the nose. After about 2-3 min. it has hardened and is ready to be removed. In one quick firm pull the wax stick pops out like a wine cork.

The amount of hair I can get off just the inner tip of the nose is just—*chef's kiss*. I often joke that it looks like a toothbrush. Then proceed to stare at it with the client, both of us shocked and amazed. Men tend to sit the worst for this service. Women always laugh. This isn't "tea," necessarily, but to see the insane amount of hair we can pluck out is just as satisfying as the hottest gossip. It's grossly satisfying. Try it, you might like it! To each their own.

~

I had a client who shared a story of her coworkers going on a trip to Las Vegas. One of the people in the group hired a "special friend" for the night. Of course, we wanted to talk further about that. After they told me how much it cost for just a hand job in Vegas, I almost considered changing careers. Just kidding, my carpal tunnel could never. Anyway, for a quick handy it was $1,300. *Get that money!* I respect the hustle. Did I ask to hear this information? No, but it was a fun, safe conversation that had both my client and I laughing. Laughter is so healing.

~

Something you should never do during salon tea or gossip, is put down another stylist. Even if the client's hair isn't as they hoped, and you are fixing it. You may not know the full story. So, it's better not to assume or gossip without them there to explain their side.

For example, what if the client went to stylist Sara last week with dark brown hair and wanted it blonde. Stylist Sara explains that it would take multiple sessions to maintain the health of the client's hair. The client is on a budget, and Sara agrees to get as much blonde in while maintaining the health of their hair, for the amount they can afford. Fast forward to the completion of the service. The results are

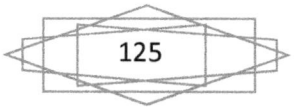

beautiful, and it is a great start to the first of several appointments to work towards their goals. The client goes home and just can't understand why it couldn't be done in one session. They begin to pick apart every aspect of the appointment and decide to call a different salon to get another appointment.

Flash forward to the second salon. The second stylist starts the consultation and is told by the client that she paid a ton of money that she didn't agree to, and that it is nothing like what she asked for. Now we know the client is full of shit, but the second stylist doesn't know the whole story. So, does stylist Sara deserve to get dragged through the mud based on just this one conversation when she isn't even there to defend herself? No, no she does not. We don't know the previous stylist's situation. We treat it as we do every client. We explain what we charge, and the realistic goals for them. It's never okay to judge the person or stylist without knowing the full situation. So, we remain like Switzerland. Neutral. Our goal is to do an outstanding service and make you feel jazzed about your hair. So as in life,

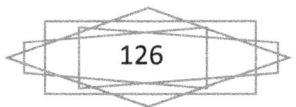

please don't spread false gossip or put down other stylist's work when you may not know the whole story.

~

Sometimes the tea is having a celebrity sit in your chair. When I was at my first salon, the lead singer of a rock band came in for a cut and wax. They were playing a show that night at the local arena. I sat them down and began my consultation. Once we had established what we were doing, I began my conversation openers. See, I had no idea who this person was, and everyone else clearly did.

I said, "So, are you from around here?"

They responded, "No, I am here for a show."

To which I respond, "Oh, cool. Who are you seeing?" The silence was deafening. After the longest pause, they said,

"No, am I performing."

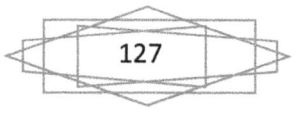

I quickly replied, "Nice, which bar or venue are you performing at?" Insert foot into mouth, or rather, I wish I had.

"The arena," he said.

"Who are you opening for?" Again, insert foot into mouth, Emily.

"I am the main act," they said.

Looking back on that, it was probably good I didn't know who they were, because I would have been nervous. Oh well, I treated them as I would have treated anyone. They got their service and were off to their show.

~

Sometimes we have situations that just make our jaws drop to the floor. People still amaze me with how crazy they can be. Especially brides— or bridezillas. I witnessed one of the worst bridezilla moments while I was still in beauty school. We worked with many bridal parties in cosmetology school. It was inexpensive for brides, and there were almost always enough

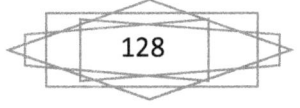

stylists to get the entire party in at the same appointment time.

"EMILY B. YOUR APPOINTMENT IS HERE!" The school speaker would blare.

I greeted a bridesmaid named Katie and took her back for her updo. The bride wanted the bridesmaids to all be in matching updos, which was typical at the time. The client showed me a photo of the updo that the bride wanted her to have. Not a problem, we completed the updo and she was happy. The instructor checked my ticket signifying that they also approved of my work, and we were good to go.

I walked Katie over to where the bride was. The bride whipped her head around and yelled, "*Fix it*! No one is going to look better than me on my wedding day!"

I said "I am sorry, I don't understand? What do you mean?"

She snapped back and said, "Mess it up. It looks better than mine does, and I won't stand for it."

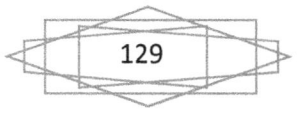

129

The bride's stylist and I looked at each other like, what-in-the-actual-F is wrong with this bride. So, I had to take Katie back to my chair and pretend to mess with it. Katie was embarrassed and kept apologizing. I didn't touch a hair though, because it was done and there was no way I was messing this poor client's hair up. That was a wild request. Brides can be wild.

~

Sometimes the gossip isn't fun or funny. It is really, really, heavy. It could be someone confiding to you about a sexual assault, abuse, or even death. That's where I need to stop and think to myself, "What kind of help can I offer?" Sometimes it is nothing but a chair to cry in. At other times, I could be a resource in helping them implement a plan of action to get them to safety.

This is where training in these areas during our education would have been so helpful. I feel like my own personal therapy sessions have turned into navigating these types of situations

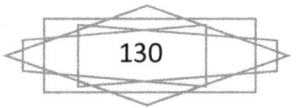

with clients. I can't come up empty handed when someone is asking for help or advice.

My therapist calls it trauma dumping. All their sadness or stressful stories cling to us like glue. I get home from the salon and my brain is zapped. I can't process anything. It takes time to wash the glue off from the day. I disassociate. I am lucky to have a great therapist. The fact that therapy is needed personally but also in my profession, makes me even more frustrated that beauty school doesn't teach psychology classes.

I need to be prepared. I have learned ways to ask if someone is safe while their abusive partner is five feet away. These things happen. We can't ignore it, but I will be damned if someone needs help, and I won't do everything in my power to assist them. There are also those that purely want to vent and do not want help or advice. So, we nod, and listen. This is the "tea" that is never fun.

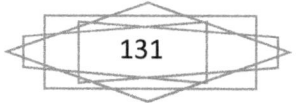

Crisis Hotlines and Resources

United Way Crisis Helpline 1-800-233-HELP

Alcoholics Anonymous; CDC National HIV and AIDS Hotline (800) 232-4636

Childhelp National Child Abuse Hotline (800) 422-4453

National Sexual Assault Hotline (800) 656-4673

National Suicide and Crisis Line: Text HOME to 741741

National Domestic Violence Hotline: (800) 799-7233

Veterans Crisis Line 988, then PRESS 1, or Text 838255

LGBTQ The Trevor Project: Text:678678 or tel:1-866-488-7386

Flaws & Challenges

There are challenges in every industry. If anyone says otherwise, they are full of bologna. Every job has frustrations, and issues that few understand, unless you have been in their shoes. The following stories give some insight into the issues we face daily, and the challenges of the profession.

~

Don't you just hate it when your favorite product is discontinued? We sure do. Whether it's supply chain issues, poor global sales, or simply out with the old, in with the new. It always sucks. It's like losing a good friend. Seriously. You have the perfect products that make your hair do

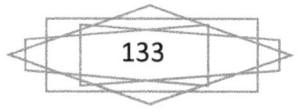

just what you want then—poof! Gone! It happens all the freaking time.

I have tried to find the products that shift the least. I also look at the ingredients, packaging, price point, company ethics, and consistency. It can be annoying for the client when products change, but we try to plan and find a suitable replacement before you even know that it is no longer available.

~

To anyone buying products at box stores, online, the grocery store or from a non-hair retail store, please do yourself a favor. Check the batch number on the product. There is a series of little printed numbers and letters that when searched, reveal the date the product was produced. If that date is past two years, it is no longer going to work correctly. Not necessarily damaging your hair, but certainly wasting your money.

Oftentimes, they have been tampered with as well. If you are not buying from a licensed retailer, such as your local stylist, then there is no

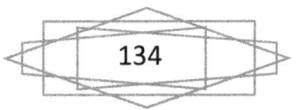

way to guarantee every ounce of it is a real, untampered, non-expired product. You know how they make knock off handbags? They do that with hair products as well. You have been warned.

~

Inflation hits us all. I can look back over the last four years and see how the cost of all our products and supplies has increased by 23%. If I go back ten years, the products have a 100% increase. It is for that reason that I made the decision to not make money off my retail. I sell it at a 10% increase from what my wholesale price is. That covers my expenses for shipping the products from the supplier. I would rather have my clients use the quality of products they need, versus getting something at the grocery store that they know nothing about or isn't even for their hair type.

If I were to charge correctly for retail, then you would be paying the same amount for your products as for your hair service. For some that may not be a problem, but for many it's not

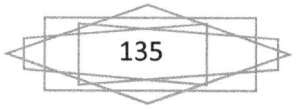

possible. I can't justify charging $40 for a can of mousse. I just can't.

I am sure I will get ripped for how I justify this, but it is my choice. I stand by providing my clients affordable, quality hair care products. Sue me.

~

There are so many people out there bashing hair stylists for how much they charge for their services. But let me provide some insight. Many don't see the struggle to find affordable health insurance, the cost is outrageous! Beyond the liability insurance we pay, there is the cost of products not only for color, or chemical services, but our entire back bar of products which we show clients how to use. Then there's the cost of rent, the cost of our credit card processing services, our booking site services. The cost of our equipment often gives people a shock: a new set of shears can be upwards of $2,000. A new dryer every year is $300. Our clippers and blades are over $500. So, things really add up. In the end, we are never

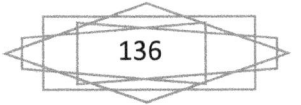

charging enough, or we are kicking ourselves for not upping rates sooner.

Let's do some math. Say you brought in $1,250/week. That's just an average. Many other areas of the world could be half that, or triple that amount, or even ten times that amount. This is just an example of an average income. So, per month, prior to taxes (yes, we must pay those too) we've made $5,000. Liability insurance is $100. Rent is $900. Products, color, and retail are $1,000 at minimum. There are other things, but those are the big ones. After all that you have roughly $3,000 left. Then take taxes out, and it's $2,200. That does not include health insurance, mind you.

Again, these are all vague numbers. You could be in the Midwest making $50 for a haircut, or on the West Coast charging $500. They know what they need to charge, and if they are booked, then they are obviously worth it, or not concerned about their rates. *Pop off Queen. Make that money!*

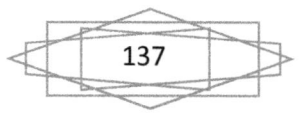

I know overseeing your own rates and not leaving it to an employer was the best choice I ever made. If you work hard and build the clientele, you are set. It sounds so easy, right? It takes consistency, skill, and professionalism. That is the secret combination. When you can only rely on yourself to be bringing the money home, you suddenly become the hardest worker in the room. You see the immediate effects of your hard work. You oversee your destiny. Cheesy, but it is that simple.

~

Learning a new color line is a real light-the-whole-house-on-fire experience. So many say, "It's a box of color. Shouldn't it be easy?" *Umm, no*. However, it pushes you to learn and grow, which is all part of the fun.

Getting to customize each client's color, formulating, and pushing the color wheel to its fullest potential is exhilarating. Each color line is so different from the next. I've easily used dozens of different color lines in my career. Some have

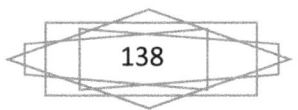

ammonia, some are ammonia free, others offer heavy opaque color, while the next line has natural multi-tonal properties. Vivid colors are in a bracket of their own, and they vary just as much. It really is trial and error sometimes. We just educate ourselves and take as many hands-on classes as possible to learn all that the color line is capable of. Education never ends!

I switched to my current color line because the previous one was causing too much irritation for my clientele's skin. It was an ammonia-based product. The product rep for the color company I used said to add Sweet'N Low sugar to the color to keep it from irritating their skin, and balance the pH of the color on the skin. I tried their suggestion, and it was effective. However, it felt so unprofessional to add Sweet'N Low sugar to a color bowl with the client staring back at me like, *Emily? Are we all seeing this? Is this normal? I trust you, but I have questions.*

I switched color lines as soon as I was able to. Best choice I could have made. I have rarely regretted changing or trying new products. I educated myself and knew what I needed to do. If I had questions, I had other stylists to brainstorm solutions with. There is nothing wrong with consulting others. They may have an idea you've never even considered. We all think and work differently. Use the wealth of knowledge that surrounds you every day. Everyone thinks differently and that is a beautiful thing. When one stylist suggests one option, another stylist might give you a completely different one. Google doesn't always have the answers, but your peers might!

~

Please Don't

Many of my clients have told me that they would love to know what they should or shouldn't do while in the salon. I know that some of these things may be obvious, but it never hurts to mention them. Think of it as a handbook for being a great client. Please:

- Don't stare at me with your eyes open while I'm shampooing your hair. It's weird.

- Don't lift your head when we're shampooing you. Relax, sit back, and let us shift your head as needed. If you lift your head, it is almost guaranteed that water will be dripping down your back beneath your shirt, because there is a gap which allows the water to escape the shampoo bowl.

- Don't be afraid to tell us you don't like our suggestions or ideas. It is your hair!

- Don't be afraid to voice your opinions at the end of the service. If you don't like how your hair turned out, tell us. I would much rather have you come back so we can change or adjust it to your liking.

- Don't be afraid to go to a different stylist. This may sound shocking, because it can feel like you are firing your stylist, but you may just want to change it up. Maybe you found someone whose schedule is more flexible. Maybe you need a different price point, or they specialize in a specific cut or color. It's completely fine to switch it up!

- Don't be afraid to tell us you prefer a quiet service. Meaning, if you want to have your hair done in peace, without the obligation

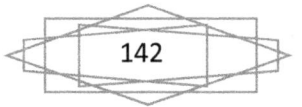

of a conversation, it's better to tell us, so we don't think you are upset with us or the service. There are lots of stylists who offer silent services. Again, it is your time, your money, your appointment.

- Don't assume we can make your hair look just like the reference picture you brought. Your face shape, texture, and density all contribute to the final look. We can work together through consultation to come to an agreement about what will be best and what adjustments should be made. Pictures help us understand the concept of what you are wanting, versus trying to explain it and being concerned we aren't on the same page. However, the final product may not match the image exactly.

- Don't ever cut your own bangs. This speaks for itself.

- Don't go out to the car for a smoke when it is ten degrees outside. The temperature will vastly affect how your hair will be processed. Heat will make it turn runny,

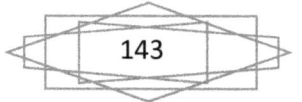

and cold temperatures will slow it down and not allow the cuticle of the hair to open and deposit the color correctly.

- Don't sit in my chair and say, "My boyfriend likes it long." News flash: it isn't their hair. Don't let your partner dictate how long, short, wavy, or straight it should be. Again, it's your hair!

- Don't assume your dry ends can be healed. There are some products to help restore some of the luster or health, but ultimately, you need to cut it, friend.

- Don't be afraid to tell me your budget. I want to do a service that is beneficial to you, that you are comfortable maintaining financially.

- Don't come in for your appointment if you are sick. If you and I are in a small studio alone, I am bound to get whatever illness you have. I wouldn't do that to you, please don't do it to me. If you are getting over something, like a cold, and are past the

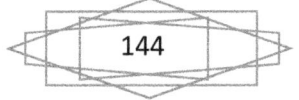

coughing and sneezing phase, you and I can both wear masks. I have them for us both if we should need it.

- Don't call me asking what times I have open, and then respond with, "Well, what about 6:00 PM?" after I have told you I only have a 2:30 PM. This may seem silly, but it happens all the time. The times I have available are as stated, and if anything changes, we can reach out to you. We often have a waitlist. Sometimes you're lucky and snag an appointment, but most often, we are fully booked. Pre-booking is the best way to ensure that you get the time and date you want.

- Don't leave it up to chance if you have a hard schedule and need to come in during a premium time, such as an evening or a weekend. Clients often book even 2-3 appointments out.

- Don't force your child to get a haircut they hate. I have had so many kids that have fought to keep their hairstyle, and then the parents demand a military cut. It puts us in an awkward spot. We must do what the parents want, they are paying for it after all, but the haircut is not on the parents. It is on the fourteen-year-old in tears, because they don't want their "Bieber Fever" haircut touched (every kid had this cut between 2008-2012). To have the parents making fun and bullying them to the point they are in tears is uncalled for. Especially in public. I can only imagine what goes on at home. Please try to come to an agreement on what you both want before coming into the salon to save us all from the trauma.

- Don't, and I mean, please *do not* say you want three layers. When layers are cut into your hair, it creates hundreds, if not thousands of micro layers. Not just three layers. If you want three layers, I will boot you out of my chair.

The infamous three-layer cut

The Hustle

Everyone hustles. Some must work harder than others. Some need to increase their income quickly due to a change in finances, and some just want that new G-Wagon. Everyone who has a goal, and really works at it, can make it a reality. If you don't have perseverance in your work ethic, I can point you to the exit door. Working for yourself really kicks that into overdrive. *Am I in control of my destiny? Yes, bitch, you really are.* That goes for life too, but work is hard! No one is going to drop money or opportunities into your lap. You may have to work seven days a week, you may have to work weekends, evenings, and miss social events. You will bust your ass ten times more when it's all on you. Will you get a lunch break? Probably not. Will you get to stop and go to the restroom? Again, probably not.

While there will always be cons to the hustle, there are also pros. Need money for groceries? You're short on the rent? You can pick up extra hours. The salon I rent from has people calling in nonstop for appointments, looking for a new stylist. That's easy money. It is a sign of a healthy and growing salon. There are always opportunities for those who want them. You just must be willing to do the work. At the end of the day if you have food in the fridge, a roof over your head, and your bills are paid, you are going to be okay.

The economy is struggling, inflation is nuts, and so many people have more than one job, even two or three. I only have one, but it's nonstop work. I am always grateful for what my job grants me, and I'm always hustling.

At the end of the day, we all need to use the golden rule. We need to respect each other and treat one another as we want to be treated. There will always be haters but remember to have

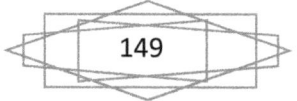

grace for every soul you meet in this world. That is a large part of the work of a hairdresser. Think about who washes your dad's hair, your mom's hair, your child's cut, who colors your partner's hair. You look at these people in your life all the time, yet they have someone else behind them, keeping in touch with them, ensuring they look and feel like their best self. Giving a good haircut supports mental wellbeing, provides emotional support, and takes physical work.

Please, the next time you see your barber, cosmetologist, or self-care guru, make sure you take note how much we have been through together. I am personally very grateful for every client I have, and every relationship we have built. We built this together and I am forever thankful for that.

I hope you enjoyed reading my diary. I hope it shows how much passion, creativity, and dedication we have for our craft. I love this career and I regret very little over the last eighteen years as a hairdresser.

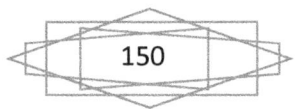

Thank you to everyone who has supported me, and to anyone who has shown their hairstylist some love. In the words of Bob Marley, "One Love." Unity. Peace. Support. Community.

The End.

~Emily

P.S.

It is a diary after all. One more story… my most favorite memory:

The funniest thing that has ever happened to me in a salon happened about eleven years ago. I was with my work besties, and it was a busy night. The waiting room was packed, and there were only three of us working. Naturally you move quicker and can't pay close attention to your surroundings. Well, my clumsy feet somehow got caught around my dryer cord. I stumbled, but caught myself, *that was a close one!* Followed by tripping again on the other curling iron cord, I had missed. Down I went. Funny, but not that funny, right? *Right.*

I forgot to mention all three of us working that night were pregnant (don't worry, this isn't a birth story). So, the two other stylists were on one side of the salon, and I was on the opposite side. When I started to fall (again, I was seven months pregnant), my dumbass thought I should put my

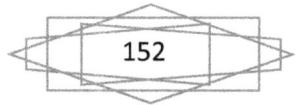

arms straight up into the air and roll across the salon floor. Why? Why did I roll across the floor?

I have no idea. It was the worst natural instinct reaction in history. *Hey silly, you are pregnant, don't try to curl up, just roll like a rolling pin across the salon floor.* The worst part was, I'd only stopped rolling once I had run into the other stylist on the other side of the salon and came to a stop. I had that much momentum going. I pulled off a great *drop* and *roll*— but not a very good *stop*.

When the girls stopped crying and laughing at what they had just witnessed, they asked if I was okay. Other people came rushing to check on me, and I was so embarrassed. *Just leave me here to die. Ugh.* Luckily, I was fine, and we still laugh so hard every time we remember it. That story encapsulates the beauty of a salon environment. Whenever you fall, you can dust yourself off and laugh about it.

P.P.S. I don't have anything else. I just had to p.p.s. something. If you got this far, thank you for humoring me.

~Emily

To my boys,

I love you and I am so thankful to have your love and support always. You are my world.

In Memory of Spotty Joe II

2002 – 2020

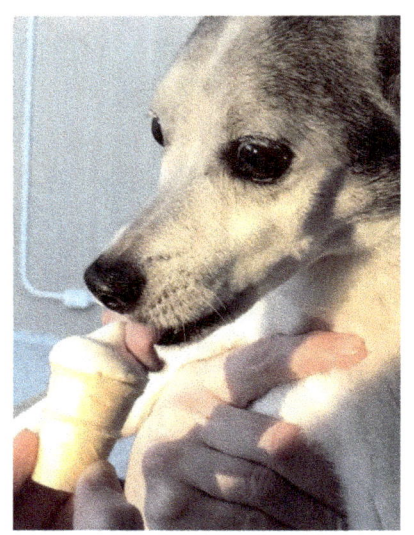